Fruyt and Chaf

Studies in Chaucer's Allegories

. . . seint Paul seith that al that writen is,
To oure doctrine it is ywrite, ywis.
Taketh the fruyt, and lat the chaf be stille.

Fruyt and Chaf

Studies in Chaucer's Allegories

By Bernard F. Huppé
and D. W. Robertson, Jr.

1963

Princeton University Press
Princeton, New Jersey

Publication of this book has been aided by
the Ford Foundation program to support publication,
through university presses, of works in the
humanities and social sciences

∴

Printed in the United States of America
by Princeton University Press, Princeton, New Jersey

TO THE MEMORY OF

Carleton Brown

A N D

George R. Coffman

Preface

THIS BOOK was first written some ten years ago when the authors shared the same office, an office famous for the sounds of good-natured altercation which echoed in the adjacent corridor and bore witness to the lively discussions of literary matters going on inside. We were frequently joined by our friend John Weld, whose deep-voiced contributions were extremely helpful in the formulation of opinions. When the authors were separated by a whim of Fortune, the book lay neglected in a hopeless collection of hastily typed pages ornamented with pencilled notes in two barely legible hands which not only crowded the spaces between the lines and the margins, but frequently spilled over on the backs of pages or on miscellaneous loose slips. As the years passed, however, the authors found that what was contained in the book and gradually added to it still seemed good to them; and in the summer of 1961 Professor Huppé undertook the Herculean labor of straightening out the manuscript. To oversimplify somewhat, this revision was in turn revised by Professor Robertson, and the changes thus made were once again smoothed out by Professor Huppé. The result now represents interpretations of Chaucer's two poems which both authors endorse heartily; and the basic ideas in it, which are the fruits of our old discussions, are genuine products of joint efforts which neither author could very well claim to be his alone.

We fully realize, having observed the reaction to an earlier product of our literary conversations, *"Piers Plowman" and Scriptural Tradition* (Princeton, 1951), that the reception of this book is likely to be mixed.

Preface

The techniques for interpreting medieval allegories are still not firmly established, and errors of detail are to be expected. But the fact that medieval statements about poetry and allegory should be taken seriously can now hardly be denied; and medieval commentaries, like those on Dante, for example, furnish a clear indication of the manner in which medieval allegories were read and understood. We hope that disagreement with our detailed interpretations may lead to a better knowledge of Chaucer's art and to a greater love for it. Chaucerians should do battle vigorously, but only that Chaucer's greater triumph may ensue. An interest in this goal unites us with all true Chaucerians, no matter how much they may disagree with what we have to say.

We wish to thank the Princeton University Research Committee for financial assistance in the preparation of this book. The Princeton University Press has been generous in its cooperation, and its readers have made many helpful suggestions. Finally, we are indebted to two whom we may perhaps best address in the words of one of Chaucer's favorite old clerks:

ei mihi, non magnas quod habent mea carmina vires,
nostraque sunt meritis ora minora tuis!

Contents

Preface / vii

I

An Approach to Medieval Poetry / 3

I I

The Book of the Duchess / 32

I I I

The Parliament of Fowls / 101

Index / 149

Fruyt and Chaf

Studies in Chaucer's Allegories

An Approach to Medieval Poetry

CHAUCER'S HUMOR and his humanity translate themselves so readily across the centuries that we are not
always aware of what in his writing we do not entirely
comprehend. This remark holds true especially for his
allegorical writings, perhaps best represented in the two
poems which are to be discussed here. Unlike *The House
of Fame*, which may be incomplete, or The Prologue to
The Legend of Good Women, which is an introduction
to a collection of stories, both *The Book of the Duchess*
and *The Parliament of Fowls* stand alone as complete
and independent allegorical works. The genre of the
two poems, the French dream allegory, is well known,
but in our view any proper understanding either of the
genre itself or of Chaucer's poems in particular may be
gained only if we are familiar with the medieval conception of the method and purpose of reading.

The application of literary theory to literature itself
may at times be an exercise of dubious value, but as allegories demanding interpretation, *The Book of the Duchess* and *The Parliament of Fowls* present excellent materials for a pragmatic test of the applicability of medie-

3

val literary ideas. Attempts to interpret the two works have not been lacking, but a confusion of many voices still exists. We do not suggest that a single or absolute interpretation of either poem is possible, nor do we pretend to reduce the complexities of artistry as great as Chaucer's to a few simple formulas. We wish merely to suggest the main outlines of what Chaucer had to say to his readers. In the process of obtaining this understanding we hope to show that the artistry of the two poems discussed is considerably more developed and skillful than critics have frequently been willing to admit. In our analyses of the poems we have sought to respect the integrity of the author. We feel that when he wrote allegory, he meant his work to be interpreted as allegory; that he chose his words carefully and with discrimination so that the appearance of carelessness or inconsistency on his part sometimes results from the negligence of his modern readers; and, finally, that Chaucer was a great comic poet who heeded what his "auctor," Macrobius says: "Philosophy does not discountenance all stories nor does it accept all"; it accepts those that "encourage the reader to good works," and rejects those that serve "merely to gratify the ear."[1] In Chaucer's work we perceive an underlying vein of philosophical seriousness—as did contemporaries like Lydgate, Scogan, Usk, Hoccleve, and "followers" like Dunbar.[2]

To the medieval poet, the exterior or surface mean-

[1] *Commentary on the Dream of Scipio,* trans. W. H. Stahl (New York, 1952), p. 84.

[2] See C. F. Spurgeon, *Five Hundred Years of Chaucer Criticism and Allusion* (New York, 1960), I, pp. x-xvii, 8-63. Cf. B. F. Huppé, *A Reading of the Canterbury Tales,* to appear shortly (S.U.N.Y. Press).

An Approach to Medieval Poetry

ing of his work frequently exhibited a deliberate obscurity. For example, when the speaker in the *De planctu naturae* of Alanus de Insulis asks Nature concerning the fictions of poets, she employs in her reply the figure of the shell and the kernel, derived from the conventions of Scriptural exegesis: "Yet, in the superficial shell of the letter, the poetic lyre sounds forth falsehood; but within, it speaks to those who hear, the secret of a higher understanding, so that the exterior shell of falseness having been cast away, the reader may discover within secretly the sweet kernel of truth."[3] Suggesting as it does the connection between the techniques of exegesis and the techniques of reading poetry, the figure is of the greatest importance, for it shows that Alanus, recognized as one of Chaucer's authorities, considered that his poetry has an aim similar to that of Scripture: in both, the fable (shell or rind) was to be considered as a mere covering for the meaning (kernel or fruit). This statement does not stand in isolation. In employing the figure of the shell and kernel Alanus was merely elaborating a commonplace which had been established by St. Augustine in his basic work on Christian literature, the *De doctrina Christiana.*[4] To illustrate what Christian writing should not be, St. Augustine cites certain verses and exclaims, "This husk shakes noisy pebbles within its sweet cover, but it pro-

[3] *PL*, 210, 451. For the figure, see C. Spicq, *Esquisse d'une histoire de l'exégèse latine au moyen âge* (Paris, 1944), p. 19. For its implications, however, and for related figures and ideas the reader should consult the volumes of Henri de Lubac, *Exégèse médiévale* (Paris 1959ff.).

[4] See H. I. Marrou, *Saint Augustin et la fin de la culture antique* (Paris, 1938), p. 413. The literary implications of the *De doctrina* are discussed by B. F. Huppé in *Doctrine and Poetry* (New York, 1959), Chapter One.

5

vides food for pigs, not men! He knows what I mean who knows the gospel."[5] The verses lack underlying truth; they sound sweet to the ear, but are in fact value-less. Although the figure of husk and kernel was to be-come, as we have said, a commonplace, its full signifi-cance cannot be understood without relation to its con-text in the literary theory developed in the *De doctrina*. To establish the background for an hypothetical recon-struction of Chaucer's view of poetry, we must begin with Augustine's indispensable work.

The theory clearly gives considerable weight to the element of meaning in literature; but this emphasis is different from that assumed in the modern conception of a "moral." Augustine wished to show that story and expression are of value only insofar as they leave the mind with a conception of fundamental doctrinal truths. He makes this point when he speaks of the difficulties in interpreting the figurative or allegorical in the Bible. "No one," he says, "doubts that things are perceived more readily through similitudes and that what is sought with difficulty is discovered with more pleasure."[6] A basic principle is established here with fateful consequences for the literature of Western Christianity. Obscurity and difficulty, whether figura-tive or allegorical, are virtues in literature because they exercise the mind so that it may grasp with enthusiasm and illumination the doctrines and mysteries of the faith. For St. Augustine, the beauty of literature re-sides precisely in the discovery of simple truth behind the variety of appearance. The attitude toward sym-bolism implied here is very different from our own, as Marrou observes: "Entre ce symbolisme et le notre

[5] *De doctrina*, 3.7.11.   [6] *Ibid*., 2.6.8.

la distance est grande, car l'image y est au service de la raison et non comme chez nous de la sensibilité; le symbole ne sert pas à exprimer une sorte de révélation *sui generis* qui échapperait à la raison discursive, mais voile simplement une vérité parfaitement définie et facile à formuler en langage clair."[7] The function of the symbol or figure is thus not to produce an intense emotional reaction but to exercise the reason. The figure of rind and kernel or, as Chaucer phrases it, fruit and chaff, implies the Augustinian theory that poetry should arouse the mind of the reader to seek truth beneath the rhetorical surface. For Augustine, Christian literature has no value apart from this function.

The implications of this profoundly simple literary doctrine were difficult for the medieval poet to escape because Augustine extended the range of symbolic values to include not only the words and events of the Bible but the whole physical universe as well. His primary concern was with the interpretation of the Bible, but for him the Bible not only contained all human wisdom; it was also the highest model of eloquence. To understand the Bible it was necessary not only to interpret figurative language but to know the properties of things, since the animals, stones, herbs, and other physical objects mentioned in the Bible have symbolic meanings.[8] Specifically to further this vital knowledge, St. Augustine called on Christian writers to prepare encyclopedic works in which whatever of human learning was pertinent to Scriptural interpretation would be collected.[9] Such writers as Isidore in his *Etymologiae*, Bede in his technical writings on grammar or mathematics,

[7] Marrou, *op.cit.*, p. 490.
[8] *De doctrina*, 2.16.23-26.
[9] *Ibid.*, 2.39.59.

Rabanus in the *De Universo*, and later writers like Bartholomeus and Berchorius were to attempt this work. In the twelfth century, the trivium was devoted to the interpretation of words, the quadrivium to the interpretation of things, a division reflecting the double task of solving in word and theory the figurative difficulties of the Bible.[10] In effect, the medieval poet was furnished with an enormous storehouse of rhetorical example and symbolic wisdom. The allegorical use of secular writings as part of human learning pertinent to Christian wisdom was defended by St. Augustine.[11] The allegorical interpretation of pagan writings is abundantly attested in the works of Fulgentius and in the commentators on Vergil and Ovid. St. Augustine's specific defense of secular writing was in effect a doorway held open for secular poets, if they wrote in accord with the allegorical model of Biblical eloquence. The medieval poet could hardly fail to write without an awareness of symbolic meaning, or of the serious purpose of poetry.

We have said that the fruit in the chaff of surface meaning consists of the essential truths of the Christian faith, and that one is led to these truths through meditation rather than through emotional intuition. Since any Christian truth must be an aspect of the New Law, the method of reading to discover truth may be explicitly described, as it is by St. Augustine: "Therefore in the consideration of figurative expressions a rule such as this will serve, that what is read should be subjected to diligent scrutiny until an interpretation contributing

[10] See G. M. Paré, A. Brunet, and P. Tremblay, *La renaissance du XIIe siècle* (Ottawa, 1933), pp. 233-236.

[11] See Marrou, *op.cit.*, pp. 495ff.

to the reign of charity is produced."[12] What St. Augustine and his successors meant by charity he states briefly: "I call 'charity' the motion of the soul toward the enjoyment of God for His own sake, and the enjoyment of one's self and of one's neighbor for the sake of God; but 'cupidity' is a motion of the soul toward the enjoyment of one's self, one's neighbor, or any corporal thing for the sake of something other than God."[13]

In operation, this concept means that the world is not to be enjoyed in itself, but to be used in furthering man's pilgrimage toward the New Jerusalem: "Suppose we were wanderers who could not live in blessedness except at home, miserable in our wandering and desiring to end it and to return to our native country. We would need vehicles for land and sea which could be used to reach our homeland, which is to be enjoyed. But if the amenities of the journey and the motion of the vehicles itself delighted us, and we were led to enjoy those things which we should use, we should not wish to end our journey quickly, and, entangled in a perverse sweetness, we should be alienated from our country, whose sweetness would make us blessed. Thus in this mortal life, wandering from God, if we wish to return to our native country where we can be blessed we should use this world and not enjoy it, so that the 'invisible things' of God 'being understood by the things that are made' may be seen, that is, so that by means of corporal and temporal things we may comprehend the eternal and spiritual."[14] Although charity and

[12] *De doctrina*, 3.15.23.
[13] *Ibid.*, 3.10.16.
[14] *Ibid.*, 1.4.4. Cf. Rom. 1.20.

9

cupidity are definable in their general functions, they are variously and obscurely represented in the actual world. For this reason a basic simplicity of doctrine placed no stifling limitations on the medieval poet. The poet's function was to express in terms of the figurative and the fabled the doctrinal truth which the homilist and the confessor presented directly. The implication of Augustine's theory for the poet influenced by it would be to set before him the aim of lifting the minds of his audience to a vivid understanding of doctrinal truth through intellectual exercise. The kind of exercising husk he employed to convey doctrine would depend on the immediate environment and intellectual status of his audience.

Without making any attempt to trace the development of the Augustinian theory in such writers as Isidore, Bede, Alcuin, Rabanus, or Scotus,[15] we may turn to a very influential treatise on literature written in the twelfth century, the *Didascalicon* of Hugh of St. Victor. This work became the standard elaboration of Augustinian literary theory. In this book the technique of discovering the kernel beneath the husk is reduced to a definite system. The husk of a literary work was for Hugh made up of the *letter* and the *sense*; the kernel was the *sentence*. Actually, this system is a description of the technique of reading developed in the schools of the twelfth century. The process is described as follows: "Exposition contains three parts: *letter*, *sense*, *sentence*. *Letter* is the rightful ordering of discourse, which indeed we call construing. *Sense* is the easy and as it were open significance which the letter

[15] See B. F. Huppé, *Doctrine and Poetry*, Chapter Two, where this influence is briefly traced.

offers at the first appearance. *Sentence* is the more profound understanding which may not be attained except through exposition or interpretation. The order of these is that the *letter* is considered first, then the *sense*, and then the *sentence*. Which having been done, the exposition is completed."[16]

Hugh gives to poetry only a secondary role as it looks toward philosophy or prepares the way toward philosophy. Among the poets Hugh includes not only the writers of comedies, tragedies, fables, and histories, but also those who, as he says, "we now call philosophers": "There are two kinds of writings. Writings of the first kind are termed the arts proper, those of the second kind are appendages to the arts. The arts are made up of those writings which are comprised under philosophy . . . grammar, dialectic, and the rest of this kind. The appendages of the arts are those which sometimes look toward philosophy; that is, which are concerned in some manner with materials outside of philosophy, and confusedly approach, or if the narrative is simple, prepare the way to philosophy. Of this kind are all the songs of the poets, as tragedies, comedies, satires, heroic and lyric verses, both iambic and, indeed, didactic verses; fables as well as histories; also the writings of those whom now we call philosophers, who are accustomed to elaborate brief material with the long circumlocutions of words, and to obscure the easy sense with intricate words, or indeed to make a picture, plundering diverse things at the same time, of many colors and forms."[17]

Thus on the level of *sense* Hugh recognizes that the

[16] *Didascalicon*, ed. C. H. Buttimer (Washington, D.C., 1939), p. 125.
[17] *Ibid.*, p. 54.

poet normally employs obscurity. But this obscurity must be placed in the service of philosophy, for poetry is the handmaiden of philosophy, not the reverse. Poetry may be properly used, Hugh continues, only if one has a knowledge of true doctrine. With such knowledge, the reader finds *sentence* arising from fiction especially memorable: "Wherefore it seems to me that the first labor must be given to the arts where the foundations of all learning are, and pure simple truth is discovered. ... Finally, the rest, if time permits, are to be studied because sometimes readers are accustomed to delight more in comic things mixed with the serious; in such readings rarity makes the good precious. Thus in the midst of a fiction we sometimes retain more eagerly the *sentence* discovered."[18] This concept is very similar to St. Augustine's concept that the true function of figurative expression is to excite the mind in a way not possible in direct address. To summarize, fiction or poetry is an adjunct of philosophy or the study of Christian wisdom. Poetry is to be distinguished from other branches of learning by its use of figurative and oblique speech. Poetry should be read carefully with three ends in view: the *letter*, the *sense*, and the *sentence*. The last of these, which is the fruit of interpretation, is the most important. Figurative and oblique fiction helps to make truth memorable, but in any event it must lead toward truth, for as St. Augustine insists, all human learning has as its purpose the movement of the soul toward charity. The importance given the poet in the Augustinian system imposes upon him the obligation always to write with the ultimate aim of promoting the Christian doctrine of charity.

[18] *Ibid.*, p. 55.

An Approach to Medieval Poetry

We have already indicated that Hugh's contemporary, Alanus de Insulis, was aware of the distinction between fruit and chaff. In the introduction to the *Anticlaudianus* there is a further illustration of the prevalence and continuity of the Augustinian tradition. Alanus shows figuratively the relative importance of *sense* and *sentence* as he considers the various degrees of possible understanding which may arise from the study of his poem: "Indeed, in this work the sweetness of the literal sense allures the puerile hearing; moral instruction will fill the advancing sense; the more acute subtlety of the allegory will sharpen the intellect approaching perfection."[19] The sweetness of fable and poetic adornment on the level of *sense* are allurements only to the senses. On the level of *sentence* the poem will appeal morally to the mind which is progressing in doctrine. And the full force of the allegory will affect the intellect approaching perfection. Moreover Alanus' figure distinguishes puerile, advancing, and mature persons. These distinctions suggest a classification of the members of his possible audience. A boy (*puer*) represents a person subject to his senses. Adolescence and youth (*proficiens*) indicate periods of discipline and training. Maturity (*perficiens*) symbolizes the approach to the divine.[20] Thus some of the auditors of

[19] *PL*, 210, 487. Cf. Hugh of St. Victor, *op.cit.*, p. 95; and Origen, *Periarchon*, quoted by Lubac, *op.cit.*, I, p. 199.

[20] Alanus has phrased his remarks so as to suggest a conflation of the traditional six ages of man into three. The figurative significance of these ages is given by Hugh of St. Victor in the *Miscellanea*, *PL*, 177, 517: "In vita hominis prima est infantia, secunda pueritia, tertia adolescentia, quarta juventus, quinta virilis aetas, sexta senectus. Prima, id est infantia, quasi quodam diluvio lubricae oblivionis orbruitur, ut non videatur in posterum, nec vestigia sui ulla relinquat. Secunda, id est pueritia,

13

the *Anticlaudianus* who perceive only the sense level are as boys. Those who see the moral significance of the poem are like growing young men. And, finally, those who discover the full *sentence* are like mature men. There is something in the poem for all of these, whether they are beginning their course of study, are advancing in it, or are completing it: "Let them therefore not dare to feel loathing for this work who, still wandering in the nurseries of a lower discipline, are nourished by the breasts of nurses. Let not those attempt to belittle this work who are undertaking the knighthood of the higher science. Let them not presume to dismiss this work who are shaking at its summit the heaven of philosophy."[21]

For those who have not subjected themselves to any intellectual discipline Alanus has nothing but contempt and desires that they not read his book. He wishes to provide food for men, not for pigs: "From this work may entrance be forbidden to those, who, given only to the mirror of the senses, do not heed the demand of reason; who, pursuing only the image of sensuality, do not desire the truth of reason, lest a holy thing be soiled, prostituted before dogs; lest pearls perish crushed under the feet of swine. . . . Senseless men should not read their own interpretation into this work, who beyond the measure of the senses cannot

---

primum de diluvio oblivionis ad sensum exiens, per superbiam erigitur, et per concupiscentiam dividitur et dispergitur. Tertia, id est adolescentia, primum per cohibitionem disciplinae circumciditur, deinde praeceptis informatur et consilio regitur. Quarta, id est juventus, servire jam cogitur, et subjicitur regimini, ut per timorem hominis divinum discat. Quinta, id est virilis aetas, post timorem hominis, ad divinum venit. Sexta, id est senectus, quasi hinc mox abitura concupiscentia futurorum trahitur."

[21] *PL*, 210, 487.

extend the course of reason, who according to the dream of imagination either recall what is seen or discuss unrecognizable fictional artifices. But those who do not allow the material of reason to rest in vicious imaginings, but dare to attempt a perception of celestial forms, should enter into my work. . . ."[22] From Alanus, Chaucer would have learned that the poet must write for those who are prepared to understand what they read on the level of the *sentence*.

He would have learned much the same thing from Dante, for Dante shows himself aware of the need to interpret his own writings on more than one level. His famous letter to Can Grande is nothing more than an exposition of this attitude. In this letter and in the *Convivio*, he speaks of two levels of discourse, the literal and the allegorical, by which he means exactly what Hugh of St. Victor called *sense* and *sentence*, or what was figuratively called shell and kernel, or chaff and fruit.[23] In the *Convivio* the allegorical level is defined and illustrated as follows: "e questo è quello che si nasconde sotto 'l manto di queste favole, ed è una veritade ascosa sotto bella menzogna: si come quando dice Ovidio che Orfeo facea con la cetera mansuete le fiere, e li arbori e le pietre a sè muovere; che vuol dire che

---

[22] *Ibid.*, 487-488.

[23] In the letter to Can Grande, ed. Toynbee (Oxford, 1920), p. 173, the levels of meaning are reduced to two: "Et primus dicitur literalis, secundus vero allegoricus, sive mysticus." Dante goes on to say that the term *allegorical* is used to include all the non-literal levels (p. 174): "Et quamvis isti sensus mystici variis appelentur nominibus, generaliter omnes dici possunt allegorici, quum sint a literali sive a historiali diversi." Cf. *Convivio*, ed. Brusnelli and Vandelli (Florence, 1934), p. 96, and p. 97, note 1. We assume the letter to Can Grande to be genuine, but are aware that the ascription is debated.

lo savio uomo con lo strumento de la sua voce faria
mansuescere e umiliare li crudeli cuori, e faria muovere a
la sua voluntade coloro che non hanno vita di scienza
e d'arte: e coloro che non hanno vita ragionevole alcuna
sono quasi come pietre."[24] The lying fables of the poets
are not lies at all, for under the fable a truth is hidden.
Dante explains here that he uses the term *allegorical* in
accordance with the usage of poets rather than in accordance with that of theologians. By this distinction he
means merely that the theologians use *allegorical* in
a technical sense to refer to one of the levels of exegetical sentence, whereas poets use it to refer to a rhetorical
trope. He is merely cautioning the reader against a
difficulty already apparent to Bede, who used the term
allegorical for rhetorical allegory to distinguish it from
what he calls the "typical" level in exegesis.[25] Dante
insists that the allegorical level must be sought by the
wise.[26]

"Fraunceys Petrak, the lauriat poet," further develops the relationship between theology and poetry
which Dante suggests in passing. As a poet, he uses the
term *allegory* in its rhetorical sense, but he insists that
there is no essential difference between theology and
poetry. They are, indeed, allies in that both are concerned with truth expressed in figure and in allegory:

[24] *Convivio*, pp. 97-98.
[25] See Halm, *Rhetores latini minores* (Leipzig, 1863), p. 617.
Bede's term achieved no general acceptance. He did not use it
himself because of the overwhelming authority of Gregory's use
of *allegorical* in the exegetical sense. Dante's remark has been
widely discussed. E.g., see C. S. Singleton, *Dante Studies, I*
(Cambridge, Mass., 1954), pp. 84-98; Richard Hamilton
Green's criticism and Singleton's reply, *Comparative Literature*,
IX (1957), pp. 118-135.
[26] *Convivio*, p. 98.

An Approach to Medieval Poetry

"Do not delimit anything thoughtlessly, for what is more foolish than to judge of unknown things? Theology, indeed, is only in the slightest manner opposed to poetry. Do you wonder? You will wonder less when I say that theology is poetry about God: Christ is sometimes called a lion, sometimes a lamb, sometimes a worm. What is this except poetry? A thousand such things you will find in the Sacred Scriptures, which it would be tedious to pursue. What, in truth, do the parables of the Savior in the Gospel utter except speech different from the sense meanings, or, as I may express it in one word, *alieniloquium*, which we are accustomed to term allegory? Moreover, with this kind of speech all poetry is covered. But poetry is subject to theology. Who denies it? The latter treats of God and of divine things; the former of gods and men. Whence in Aristotle we read that the first poets theologized."[27] Petrarch here expresses clearly what we have seen to be traditional Augustinian principles. The word *alieniloquium* he uses for allegory is to be found in Isidore's *Etymologiae*, as is his etymological definition of theology as poetry about God.[28] His definition of allegory is that of Donatus, but may be found in St. Augustine, in Bede, or in Isidore.[29] Petrarch makes casual reference to the *sense* as a covering for the *sentence* when he says that all poetry is *covered* with allegorical speech. The subject matter of poetry is different from that of theology, but the two disciplines are similar in technique.

[27] *Familiari*, ed. Rossi, Book x, letter 4.
[28] 1.37.22 (Lindsay): "Allegoria est alieniloquium. Aliud enim sonat, et aliud intellegitur."
[29] See Keil, *Grammatici latini* (Leipzig, 1864), IV, p. 401; Halm, *op.cit.*, p. 16; St. Augustine, *Enn. in Ps. CIII*, 13; and the definition from Isidore in the preceding note.

17

An Approach to Medieval Poetry

It is also clear that Petrarch's defense of poetry against the objections of his monastic brother Gerard implies that the themes which poetry conceals are not inconsistent with theological ideals.

But in Chaucer's favorite "source," Boccaccio, specifically in the *Genealogia deorum,* we find perhaps the most elaborate and vigorous statement of the traditional theory of literature. Boccaccio considers at length the relationship between the Bible and secular literature suggested by his master Petrarch. Poetry comes, he says, from the bosom of God. Good poetry is like the Old Testament in the techniques of exposition and implication it uses. He distinguishes four kinds of fiction. The first is concerned with brutes or inanimate things which converse. The second apparently mixes fiction and truth, as does a considerable body of poetry. The third is more like history than fiction, as are the narratives of Vergil or Homer. The fourth is without value because it contains no truth of any kind. He replies to those who would condemn the first three poetic fictions, by showing their identity with fictions found in the Bible. Holy Writ contains, for example, a description of an assembly of trees. If the attackers of poetry condemn the second type of fiction, they will perforce reject the whole sacred body of the Old Testament. He continues:

"God forbid, since the writings of the Old Testament and the writings of the poets seem as it were to keep step with each other, and that too with respect to the methods of their composition. For where history is lacking, neither one concerns itself with the superficial possibility, but what the poet calls fable or fiction our theologians have named figure. The truth of this may be seen by fairer judges than my opponents, if they will but weigh in a true scale the outward literary semblance of the visions of Isaiah, Ezekiel, Daniel, and other sacred writers on the one hand, with the outward literary semblance of the fiction of poets on the other. If they find any real discrepancy in their methods, either of implication or of exposition, I will accept their condemnation. If they condemn the third form of fiction, it is the same as condemning the form which our Savior Jesus Christ, the Son of God, often used when He was in the flesh, though Holy Writ does not call it 'poetry,' but 'parable'; some call it 'exemplum,' because it is used as such. I count as nought their condemnation of the fourth form of fiction, since it proceeds from no consistent principle, nor is fortified by any reinforcement of the arts, nor carried logically to a conclusion. Fiction of this kind has nothing in common with the work of the poets, though I imagine these objectors think poetry differs from it in no respect."[30]

The first three types of poetry are all "allegorical" in the general sense of the word, and all of them find precedent in Scriptural example. Again, the character of the kernel beneath the shell of poetry is implied in the statement that it comes "from the bosom of God." Poetry is thus defended for its meaningfulness and for its relationship in method to Scripture. The Augustinian assertion that Scripture is the model of Christian rhetoric is implicit in Boccaccio's remarks.

Elsewhere, Boccaccio emphasizes the meaningfulness of poetry. He develops at length the point that poetry has as its purpose not entertainment but learning. The

---

[30] Osgood, *Boccaccio on Poetry*, pp. 49-50. Boccaccio here rests on the Augustinian distinction between useful and useless human institutions, *De doctrina*, 2.39.

only justification for fictional discourse rests in its underlying meaning. This is another way of saying, as Hugh of St. Victor had said, that poetry looks toward philosophy: "But they [the detractors of poets] may object . . . fiction is just that—idle nonsense. True enough, if the poet had intended to compose a mere tale. But I have time and time again proved that the meaning of fiction is far from superficial. Wherefore, some others have framed this definition of fiction (*fabula*);⌈fiction is a form of discourse, which, under guise of invention, illustrates or proves an idea; and, as its superficial aspect is removed, the meaning of the author is clear.⌋If, then, sense is revealed from under the veil of fiction, the composition of fiction is not idle nonsense."[31] Those who deny that poets intend a hidden meaning in their poetry are, Boccaccio says, fools: "Some of the railers are bold enough to say, on their own authority, that only an utter fool would imagine the best poets to have hidden any meaning in their stories; rather, they have invented them just to display the great power of their eloquence, and show how easily such fables may bring the injudicious mind to take fiction for truth. O the injustice of men! O what absurd dunces!"[32]

Like Alanus, Boccaccio was aware that his theory of poetry places a definite obligation upon the reader.⌈If a reader fails to see the hidden meaning, it is his own fault because⌋"when things perfectly clear seem obscure, it is the beholder's fault."[33] In this passage Boccaccio defends obscurity in poetry on traditional grounds.⌈It prevents the truth from being made vulgar, and it chal- lenges the reader to intellectual effort, so that the under-

[31] *Ibid.*, p. 48.   [32] *Ibid.*, p. 52.   [33] *Ibid.*, p. 59.

An Approach to Medieval Poetry

lying truth, once it is discovered, is more precious. With regard to the first point, Boccaccio recalls St. Augustine's figure of the husks fit only for pigs, saying, "For we are forbidden by divine command to give that which is holy to dogs, or to cast pearls before swine."[34] As we have seen, this is almost exactly the language of Alanus on the same subject. Boccaccio supports the thesis that intellectual effort in the discovery of poetic truth is desirable, employing three quotations from St. Augustine to the effect that such effort is desirable in the study of the Bible. If the Holy Spirit uses the method of veiled statement, Boccaccio insists, certainly this method is suitable for poetry. A final remark quoted from Petrarch sums up the idea of pleasure in intellectual discovery: "As saith Francis Petrarch in the Third Book of his *Invectives*, contrary to my opponents' supposition, 'Such majesty and dignity are not intended to hinder those who wish to understand, but rather propose a delightful task, and are designed to enhance the reader's pleasure and support his memory. What we acquire with difficulty and keep with care is always the dearer to us.' "[35]

As we have seen, such aesthetic pleasure was prominently mentioned in the *De doctrina*; its value was later emphasized by Hugh of St. Victor. The intellectual exercise involved in obtaining the fruit beneath the chaff may be severe, so that reading poetry involves considerable patience; Boccaccio continues: "But I repeat my advice to those who would appreciate poetry, and unwind its difficult involutions. You must read, you must persevere, you must sit up nights, you must inquire, and exert the utmost power of your mind. If

[34] *Ibid.*, p. 62.   [35] *Ibid.*, pp. 61-62.

21

one way does not lead to the desired meaning, take another; if obstacles arise, then still another; until, if your strength holds out, you will find that clear which at first looked dark. For we are forbidden by divine command to give that which is holy to dogs, or to cast pearls before swine."[36]

The closing Scriptural allusion, already referred to above, makes clear the nature of the truth to be discovered. As St. Augustine said, "What is read must be diligently turned over in the mind until an interpretation is found that promotes the reign of charity." Boccaccio's theory of poetry is clearly and unmistakably an elaboration of the central ideas of the *De doctrina*. As for the significance of these ideas, we may quote an observation from Professor Osgood's introduction: "This allegorical theory of poetry, deriving from the Ancients, and sustained from early medieval times by a naturally strong inclination to symbolism and allegory, supports the allegorical quality of literature and art from Prudentius to Spenser. Nor is it confined only to formal allegory such as the *Divine Comedy*, but suspects and seeks ulterior meaning in all art and poetry worthy of the name."[37]

If the translation of the *Roman de la Rose* was one of his apprentice tasks, Chaucer early faced the problem of translating Jean de Meun's frequent uses of the figure of the shell and the kernel. One example of many appears in a description of an heretical work:

> Or vous ai dit dou sen l'escorce,
> Qui fait l'entencion repondre,
> Or en vueil la moele espondre. (11858-11860)

[36] *Ibid.*, p. 62.
[37] *Ibid.*, pp. xxxviii-xxxix.

An Approach to Medieval Poetry

Again in his translation of Boethius, Chaucer encountered passages where the Augustinian concept of the fundamental importance of the *sentence* is expressed. For example, Philosophy insists that she is not interested in the library walls (the shell), but in their sentence (the kernel): "So that I seie that the face of this place ne moeveth me nought so mochel as thyn owene face, ne I ne axe nat rather the walles of thy librarye, apparayled and wrought with yvory and with glas, than after the sete of thi thoughte, in which I put nought whilom bookes, but I putte that that maketh bokes wurthy of prys, or precyous, that is to seyn the sentence of my bookes."[38]

According to the authorities, *sentence* is of primary importance in poetry. The concept of the *sentence* is in itself indicative of a relation between Scripture and poetry. The three levels—letter, sense, and sentence— are borrowed from Scriptural exposition. It is not unnatural to assume that poets borrowed not only the techniques of Scripture but also the standard images developed in Scripture: images like the "lion," "lamb," or "worm" mentioned by Petrarch. There can be no doubt of the relationship to Scripture of such poems as *The Divine Comedy* or *Piers Plowman*. *Piers Plowman* enforces the relationship by abundant citation of Scripture and by admonition to consult the gloss. As we have sought to show elsewhere, the interpretation of the poem is aided by an understanding of Biblical symbolism. Scriptural citations in *Piers Plowman* are not decorative or macaronic; they are signposts giving directions to the underlying meaning. On the other hand, there are poems like the two here under discussion,

[38] I, Pr. v, p. 327 (Robinson's text, 2 ed., the base of all subsequent quotations from Chaucer).

23

The Book of the Duchess and *The Parliament of Fowls*, where Scripture is not quoted, although it is reflected in some lines. Between these extremes stands such a poem as the *Vita nuova*, which, as C. S. Singleton has shown, makes central use of theological or Biblical symbolism, although Scripture is infrequently quoted.[39] Where Scripture is not directly cited, the problem of interpretation becomes more difficult, but no less than in *Piers Plowman* reference to Biblical symbolism may serve as a guide to the underlying meaning of poems in which Scripture is not directly cited. The medieval reader had available for his interpretation of poetry a body of more or less standard imagery. It was afforded in abundance by the commentators on Scripture, whose work was not only digested in compendia of various kinds but made available to a very wide public in sermons, as is evident in standard collections of homiletic materials such as John Bromyard's *Summa praedicantium*. Even a person who could not read at all would have a large fund of Scriptural imagery brought to him through the liturgy and through the sermons he heard, so that the poems, which he also heard, need not have been altogether beyond his comprehension. Medieval poetry in general may be thought of in this respect as being in the direct tradition of the very earliest Latin Christian poets whose source of inspiration was the Bible.

By the time of Chaucer and Boccaccio the common fund of Scriptural imagery had been expanded in various ways. The book of God's creation was read in exactly the same way as the book of God's word, so that values on the level of *sentence* were given to animals, birds, fish, trees, and stones not found in the Bible.

[39] See *An Essay on the Vita Nuova* (Cambridge, Mass., 1949).

An Approach to Medieval Poetry

For example, Alexander Neckam attributes symbolic values to the squirrel, even though there is no squirrel in the Scriptures. Other materials were afforded by classical poetry. The classical heroes and deities acquired new meanings as the works in which they appeared were interpreted "allegorically" in the great medieval quest for God's intention. The deities were systematically interpreted in such treatises as Ridewall's *Fulgentius metaforalis*, as the commentary on Ovid by Walsingham, as the *Ovide Moralisé*, or in exegetical works like those of Holkot. In Scriptural interpretation a favorite device was the creation of "etymologies" for words to show their higher significances. This process was indelibly impressed on the medieval tradition by the *Etymologiae* of Isidore of Seville, much of which was elaborated with a more definite Scriptural background in the *De universo* of Rabanus Maurus. The technique was borrowed by the poets and applied especially to proper names. A very obvious example appears in the Prologue to the *Second Nun's Tale*, where Chaucer gives various "etymologies" for the name *Cecile*. These are not to be thought of as alternative linguistic conjectures, but as a series of equally valid elaborations on the *sentence* of the name. If names from the Bible or elsewhere could be treated in this way, it was also possible to invent new names or to reinterpret old ones on the same principles. Much of the allegory in Boccaccio's *Eclogues* is developed in this fashion and the method is responsible for Petrarch's "Laura."[40] Finally, figures of all kinds were elaborated and given new shades of meaning in literature itself. A well-known poem like *The Romance of the Rose* could begin a

[40] On the Eclogues, see Boccaccio's own explanation, *Opere latine minori*, ed. Massera (Bari, 1928), pp. 216-221.

whole tradition of figurative values. For purposes of developing his *sentence* clearly and consistently but not too obviously the medieval poet thus had at his disposal a wide range of symbolic materials and techniques, all basically Scriptural in origin.

We may assume with some security that the medieval audience, particularly one with pretensions to culture, would be incomparably more familiar with the imagery of the Scriptures than we are. But in spite of this familiarity, the task of interpreting an allegorical poem could not have been transparently simple. Scriptural images frequently have many values, and sometimes two or even three of these values are implied simultaneously. In addition, most of the common symbols have both "good" and "evil" connotations.[41] A medieval symbol, like a coin, has two sides, and it is not always easy to determine which side a poet intends. He may, as a matter of fact, imply both. Finally, a symbol may have several seemingly unrelated values arising from quite different but authoritative interpretations of Scriptural passages. A poem is thus frequently made up of a series of variables. It is the task of the reader or listener to fix these variables in such a way that the result is coherent and leads to an acceptable *sentence*. Fortunately, it is often possible to fix one or more of the variables from the context of the poem. It remains then to make the rest of them consistent with these. For the modern reader, to whom the techniques of medieval symbolism are strange and obscure, the analysis of a medieval poem may become a difficult task indeed.

The modern reader cannot, of course, recapture the fleeting connotations which enriched a poem for the medieval audience. But beginning with the necessary

[41] See St. Augustine, *De doctrina*, 3.25.36.

assumption that the medieval poet intended to be meaningful, the modern reader can discover at least the basic pattern of meaning which underlies words and things used figuratively. To recapture the poetic perception which the medieval audience could gain from mere reflection, the modern reader must resort to the very unpoetic task of dictionary searching, to ascertain the symbolic context of key words or concepts in a poem. To aid us we have a very valuable short cut in the *répertoires exégetiques*, as Father Spicq calls them.[42] These were essentially symbolic dictionaries giving levels and varieties of meaning taken in the context of the glosses on the Bible. Dom Wilmart describes them as: "répertoires alphabétiques, dans lesquels les termes 'equivoques' de la Bible, ou censés tels, sont expliqués et discutés avec plus ou moins d'insistance et selon des méthodes variées: tantôt dans un dessein d'instruction privée ou d'édification, tantôt pour faciliter les tâches de l'enseignement officiel, tantôt enfin avec l'intention avouée de fournir une aide commode aux sermonnaires. Ces recueils, qui portèrent communément le nom significatif de *Distinctiones* et jouirent, pour la plupart, d'un grand crédit, sont tombés dans un oubli profond, quoique les exemplaires abondent encore; ils mériteraient sans doute d'être classés et examinés, afin qu'on saisît mieux l'activité intellectuelle ou, en tout cas, les preoccupations de nos ancêtres à l'egard de l'Écriture."[43] We have made use of the three which are published in the Patrologia: the *Distinctiones* of Alanus de Insulis, the *Allegoriae in sacram scripturam* wrongly attributed to Rabanus, and to a lesser degree the

[42] Spicq, *op.cit.*, pp. 175-177.
[43] "Un répertoire d'exégèse composé en angleterre vers le début du XIII siècle," *Mémorial Lagrange* (Paris, 1940), p. 308.

Gregorianum of Garnerius, both an encyclopedia after the manner of Rabanus' *De universo*, and a lexical index to Gregory's *Moralia*. We have made use also of later works whose content is essentially similar but more highly developed: Bartholomeus' *De proprietatibus rerum*, Berchorius' *Repertorium* and *Reductorium Morale*, Bromyard's *Summa Praedicantium*, and so on. But the earlier works contain the root of the tradition and, in some ways, its most authoritative expression. Our references in the notes indicate traditional meanings, not "sources." When Father Beichner's edition of the *Aurora* of Petrus Riga appears, it may be possible to enrich these annotations with materials from a source which Chaucer mentions. The selections printed in J. B. Pitra's *Spicilegium Solesmense* are not extensive enough to be of much use.

The glosses, handbooks, encyclopedias, and other guides to symbolic meanings provide us with a set of symbolic referents, but as Hugh of St. Victor said in the *Didascalicon*, it is necessary also to know something of basic doctrine. For us, this means that it is necessary to learn something of the principal tenets of medieval theology. A knowledge of modern Christian doctrine is not sufficient, since the Reformation and the Council of Trent drastically modified many medieval attitudes. For our purposes, it is impossible to recreate fully the learning and understanding of a medieval scholar, or even that of a fairly intelligent medieval layman. We must use short cuts as best we may. Among works which may be regarded as fundamental, the most convenient for reference is the *Sententiae* of Peter Lombard, which was for over three centuries the standard textbook of theology. It represents for the most part the best and most widely accepted fundamental doctrine of the later Middle Ages. For philosophical as opposed to theological principles, the *De consolatione* of Boethius is indispensable. It was not only popular among the learned, but was translated into all the important vernaculars. The notion sometimes held in modern times that Boethius may not have been a Christian did not disturb our medieval forefathers: The commentators, like Nicholas Trivet, found his work consistent with sound Augustinian doctrine.

The writings of the Fathers, especially those of Augustine, Jerome, Gregory, and Bede, are always authoritative, regardless of special tradition. Basic exegetical principles, relating theology to the study of Scripture and of literature, may be found in St. Augustine's *De doctrina* and in Hugh of St. Victor's *Didascalicon*. These works establish the principles which preserved medieval symbolism from the subjectivity of modern symbolism. One fact which it is always necessary to bear in mind is that although medieval theology displays a truly remarkable continuity of tradition, it was always changing and growing. The thirteenth century, for example, witnessed a remarkable growth of pastoral theology which manifests itself chiefly in conciliar decrees issued to implement the decrees of the Fourth Lateran Council. A given poem frequently reflects a definite stage in this chronological development. The solutions which we gain when we interpret the symbols in a poem should be checked against the basic concepts of Christian theology and philosophy, with special reference where possible to current ideas. The survival of vernacular poetry containing heretical doctrines is extremely unlikely, certain modern interpretations of medieval poems notwithstanding.[44] We may assume, unless there is direct and unmistakable evidence to the contrary, that most medieval poets were men of considerable intellectual integrity and orthodoxy. A vernacular poem was not an effective medium for the propagation of original theological ideas.

Having some external check on unlikely interpretation through a knowledge of the basic principles of medieval theology, philosophy, and exegesis, we must still approach any given vernacular work with caution. As Boccaccio points out, some works deal with events happening in the real world; others mix accounts of events with fancy, as do visions. Dream visions like *The Romance of the Rose* are by definition to be interpreted completely as "allegories." In such visions the sense level is dependent on the underlying meaning. Characters act in accordance with the demands of meaning, not in accordance with the logic of external events. An important problem in the interpretation of allegory consists in avoiding the temptation to explain the sense level in the illusion that it is the level of *sentence*. But where we deal with a parable or exemplum, to use Boccaccio's terms, we must remember that there is a logic of external events which governs the action, so that the *sentence* is often based on suggestions rather than on closely knit symbolic details. Since both *The Book of the Duchess* and *The Parliament of Fowls* are dream allegories, our concern in the present study is with the first problem. The interpretation of the two poems which we advance in this study suggests itself to us as being consistent with the details of the poems themselves. It is possible, or, indeed probable, that since

[44] Diego Zorzi's study, *Valori religiosi nella letterature provenzale* (Milan, 1954), offers a good illustration of this point.

the analysis of literary iconography is a relatively new discipline, we may have erred in detail. Nevertheless, it is our contention that the general conclusions advanced lead to a new understanding of the poems as integrated works of art. We hope that whatever errors or misconceptions may appear in the succeeding chapters may be corrected in the near future by more searching exposition based on a wider and deeper knowledge than our own.

II

The Book of the Duchess

THE BOOK OF THE DUCHESS begins with an elaborate picture of a man made sleepless through unfulfilled desire. His loss of sleep makes him idle, indifferent to good or evil, and above all full of sorrowful imaginings. Death, he thinks, will soon result from his unnatural state, for the spirit of life is dead within him. In his "mased" or irrational condition,[1] he is so confused by phantasies that he is unable to decide "what is best to do" or to determine the cause of his sleeplessness. In Froissart's *Paradys d'Amours*, from which Chaucer probably developed the introduction to *The Book of the Duchess*, the speaker specifically declares himself to be a lover languishing for his mistress;[2] but Chaucer's speaker says that if men ask him why he is sleepless, he will be unable to answer. He knows merely that one physician can cure him, and that the physician seems impossibly beyond his reach:

> I holde hit be a sicknesse
> That I have suffred this eight yeer,
> And yet my boote is never the ner;

[1] In *The Harrowing of Hell*, 247, "mased" is an alliterative synonym of "madde."

[2] Ed. Scheler, lines 1-12.

32

For ther is phisicien but oon
That may me hele; but that is don. (36-40)

The professed ignorance of the speaker presents a problem to the reader, particularly about the identification of the one physician. On the one hand, the image of the lady as the only physician to her lover's discomfort is traditional. On the other hand, the image of Christ the Physician represents an even earlier and more pervasive tradition. A similar ambiguous clue is afforded by the eight years' malady, which may simply indicate the temporal extent of the lover's suffering, or, with reference to the Physician, Christ, it may be a specific reflection of an eight years' malady found in the New Testament, that of Aeneas in the Acts of the Apostles. The eight years' malady of Aeneas is elaborately glossed. Aeneas himself is taken to represent humanity; his malady of eight years symbolizes earthly delight which is cured in the name of Christ, the Physician.[8]

[8] Acts 9.33-34. For the interpretation, see Bede, *PL*, 92, 965: "Aeneas iste genus significat humanum, infirmorum prius delectatione languescens, sed apostolorum opere et ore sanatum. Quia etenim mundus ipse quatuor plagis sublimatur, et cursus saeculi annuis quatuor temporibus variatur, quicunque praesentia labentiaque gaudia complectitur, quasi bis quaternario annorum numero, grabato sternitur enervis. Grabatum quippe est ipse segnities, ubi requiescit animus aeger et infirmus, id est, in voluptate corporis et omni delectatione saeculari. *Aenea, sanet te Dominus Jesus Christus. Surge et sterne tibi.* Quem de paralypsi curaverat, mox surgere et sternere sibi praecepit, spiritualiter insinuans ut quisque fidei solidamentum in corde perceperit, non solum torporem, in quo fessus jacuerat, discutiat, sed etiam bona opera, in quibus requiescere valeat, paret." This explanation is repeated in the *Glossa ordinaria*, *PL*, 114, 449. The figure of Christ the Physician is sufficiently commonplace. The number "eight" frequently suggests Christ, who brings about a cure for the languor described by Bede.

In the biblical figure of the Physician, the audience is given one way of understanding the portrait of the sleepless man. He is one who knows that there is but one Physician, but he has lost access to Him because he has been so overcome by a temporal loss that he has almost fallen into despair. He sees, for the moment, no way to the "sleep" or quiet of life which he knows that God alone can give him.[4] In short, the reader is made aware that the temporal loss suffered by the poet is

---

See Isidore, *Liber numerorum, PL*, 83, 189; or Bede, *Hexameron, PL*, 91, 149 and 162. For the idea that the sorrow of the *persona* at the opening of the poem is sorrow for Blanche, and not for some conjectural lost mistress, see Marshall W. Stearns, "A Note on Chaucer's Attitude Toward Love," *Speculum*, XVII (1942), pp. 570-574. R. S. Loomis, *MLN*, LIX (1944), pp. 178-180, thinks that Chaucer was simply being conventional. Chaucer had probably read Henry of Lancaster's *Livre de Seyntz Medicines* and was thus thoroughly aware of the Scriptural connotations of figures like "malady," "physician," and so on.

[4] *Quies vitae* is one of the standard allegorical meanings of "sleep." E.g., see *Allegoriae in sacram scripturam, PL*, 112, 913. The fact that "sleep" has a number of other meanings equally commonplace need not be disturbing, since they do not fit the context of our poem. To indulge for a moment in an analogy, the fact that a word may have various meanings does not imply that it is useless for poetic purposes. The meaning intended is usually clear from the context. On the source of true rest, see St. Augustine, *De catechizandis rudibus*, 16: "Nam et in hac vita homines magnis laboribus requiem quaerunt et securitatem, sed pravis cupiditatibus non inveniunt. Volunt enim requiescere in rebus inquietis et non permanentibus; et quia illae tempore subtrahuntur et transeunt, timoribus et doloribus eos agitant, nec quietos esse permittunt." This is, of course, one of the lessons of Boethius in the *De consolatione*. The poet or speaker at the beginning of Chaucer's poem has been disturbed by a temporal loss.

very great, a measure of the worth of the subject of eulogy, Blanche the Duchess, so sorely mourned by one of her followers.

In his imaginary self-portrait, Chaucer stresses his idleness. He suggests thereby that for one who, like himself, has lovingly served Blanche, her loss may lead to an almost inconsolable bereavement, that is, to the condition of *tristitia*,[5] the nature of which may be suggested by John the Scot's definition of Hades as "tristitia vel deliciarum privatio."[6] *Tristitia* prevents the speaker from performing any good works and even from desiring to do so. To him, as well as to her other mourners, Blanche had presumably been a source of spiritual inspiration, one among those who, with Queen Philippa, helped to instil ideals of courtesy and chivalry in Edward's court, which, for a time, was the most brilliant in Europe. But just as love for Blanche in life inspired noble action in her friends and admirers, so also that love may be turned toward even greater inspiration at her death. The problem of the poem is to show how this "conversion" may be effected. And the solution is suggested at the opening by the eight years' malady and by the play on the idea of the physician.

Continuing in his "mased" search for consolation, the speaker, lacking sleep, considers various kinds of slothful distraction. A French book, or "romance," seems better game than chess or tables. It is an ancient book, translated and rhymed by poets who wrote "while men loved the lawe of kinde," or, that is, while they re-

---

[5] See Chaucer's *Parson's Tale*, p. 297 : "Now comth wanhope, that is despeir of the mercy of God, that comth somtyme of to muche outrageous sorwe. . . ."

[6] *De div. nat.*, PL, 122, 954. Hell involves the ultimate "despeir of the mercy of God."

spected Nature, whose precepts are violated by the speaker's slothful condition. He finds in the book stories about kings and queens which seem irrelevant to his condition and hence trivial. But one story seems "a wonder thing," perhaps because it is relevant to him in mirroring and commenting upon his own grief. It reveals one possible consequence of his despairing grief, which he has, in fact, already considered, that is, self-destruction. When her husband, Seys, is lost at sea, Alcyone laments for him inordinately. She vows to her god that she will never eat bread until she hears from Seys. In answer to her prayer, Juno sends a messenger to Morpheus, who lives in a dark, barren cave, demanding that he bring the body of Seys to Alcyone in a dream. When Seys comes to her through Morpheus, he tells her that her sorrow is futile:

> My swete wyf,
> Awake! let be your sorwful lyf!
> For in your sorwe there lyth no red.
> For, certes, swete, I nam but ded;
> Ye shul me never on lyve yse.
> But, goode swete herte, that ye
> Bury my body, for such a tyde
> Ye mowe hyt fynde the see besyde;
> And farewel, swete, my worldes blysse!
> I praye God youre sorwe lysse.
> To lytel while oure blysse lasteth! (201-211)

The message is essentially philosophical; it urges Alcyone to awaken from worldly concern and to act as a true widow should, realizing herself to be "bereft of every aid except that of God alone."[7] But Alcyone, who is blind to truth of this kind, cannot understand him:

[7] Alanus, *Distinctiones, PL,* 210, 1002. Chaucer's version of

36

With that hir eyen up she casteth
And saw noght. (212-213)

She continues to lament, and dies on the third day. The
selection of this story from among the others in his book
may indicate that the speaker is in a parallel situation
of bereavement. If he too had a vision, would he be
able to understand a message like that of Seys?

At the point where Alcyone is unaware of the fate of
her husband, saying that she will not eat bread until
she hears certainly of him, the speaker pauses to attest
his sympathetic grief for her:

> Such sorwe this lady to her tok
> That trewly I, which made this book,
> Had such pitee and such rowthe
> To rede hir sorwe, that, by my trowthe,
> I ferde the worse al the morwe. (95-100)

Alcyone's grief was at first like that of David before
he knew certainly the fate of his first son by Bathsheba.
He mourned and refused to eat before the boy died, but
afterward, unlike Alcyone, when he knew that his son
was dead, he threw off his mourning and broke bread,
declaring to his servants the futility of further lament.
His statement is not unlike that of Seys in its import
(2 Kings 12. 22-23): "And he said: While the child
was yet alive, I fasted and wept for him: for I said:
Who knoweth whether the Lord may not give him to
me, and the child may live? But now that he is dead,
why should I fast? Shall I be able to bring him back
any more? I shall go to him rather: but he shall not re-

---

the story should be contrasted with the original, where Cey
says (*Met.* 11.669), "da lacrimas lugubriaque indue." In effect,
the sense of the original is reversed.

37

turn to me." Death has effectively removed all justification for further show of grief.

Alcyone, on the contrary, continues to lament after she has learned the truth, refusing consolation. At first glance, for the speaker to fare the worse "al the morwe after" in thinking of her sorrow seems inconsistent. Since the morrow would be after he had awakened from the dream which he recounts in his own poem, he betrays inordinate sympathy for an irrational grief, and he appears to be left sorrowful rather for Alcyone than for the lamented Blanche. These inconsistencies disappear if we remember that one should not grieve for a true Christian who has gone to his reward, although one may grieve, but not inordinately, over the lamentable fate of a misled sinner. As St. Jerome explains in one of his consolatory epistles, "David justly lamented the death of his son who was a parricide; but afterward, when he could not bring it about that his other son might live, he did not lament his death because he knew that he had not sinned."[8] Chaucer's statement of grief over Alcyone can represent a foreshadowing of the consolation he attains at the end of the poem. Seys brings a philosophic message of comfort which that other "mased" creature, Alcyone, chooses not to hear; in consequence, it is her sorrow which is lamentable, not the death of Seys, the occasion for her grief. The application of the *sentence* of her fate to the plight of the grieving poet is clear. He must regard his own loss as something other than a blow of adverse Fortune, and he must learn to understand the relevance of Seys' message to his own situation.

In spite of his statement that he grieved for Alcyone

[8] *Epistolae*, ed. Hilberg (Vienna, 1910), Pars I, 301. See also Hugh of St. Victor, *PL*, 177, 495.

"al the morwe aftir," the poet indicates no immediate, overwhelming concern for Alcyone's plight. He merely wonders about any god who can cause a man to sleep, and speaks in "game," though his mood is not playful. When he has read his Ovidian story, he makes a joking vow to Morpheus or to Juno or to "som wight elles," and falls immediately to sleep. The fact that he prays to Morpheus "in game" and at the same time asserts that he knows only one God shows that he does not take the personages to whom he prays seriously as deities. Whatever power they have to "make men sleep" is not their own, but God's. Their power is illusion. The sleep of the poet, if it is to provide rest from his torment, must result from a deeper understanding of the story of Seys and Alcyone, which he had read "wel" and "overloked everydel."

Alcyone prays to Juno for help:

> Helpe me out of thys distresse,
> And yeve me grace my lord to see.
> Soone, or wite wher-so he be,
> Or how he fareth, or in what wise,
> And I shal make you sacrifise,
> And hooly youres become I shal
> With good wille, body, herte, and al. (110-116)

Whatever meaning Juno may have in this context, it is clear that Alcyone is interested only in what she may see or hear and not in the intangible but nevertheless real virtues which Seys may have had. In Christian terms, her prayer is in substance idolatrous.[9] In terms of pagan wisdom like that found, for example, in Cic-

[9] Cf. Chaucer's *Parson's Tale*, line 859: "Certes, be it wyf, be it child, or any worldly thyng that he loveth biforn God, it is his maumet, and he is an ydolastre."

ero's *De amicitia*, a work which Dante praised for its
efficacy in consolation, it is unreasonable. Alcyone is subject to "fantasye" in her solicitude and is therefore not
in a position to heed any reasonable counsel her vision
may suggest to her.[10] As a result of her plea to Juno she
falls into a "ded slepe," a sleep of spiritual torpor, reflected in the details of the dark vision of the rocky cave
of Morpheus.[11] If his habitation suggests the mind, it

[10] On "phantasies," see St. Augustine, *Epistolae*, 7, to Neb-
ridius. The most widely known interpretation of the story of
Ceyx during Chaucer's maturity was probably that which appears in Holkot's commentary on Wisdom. W. A. Pantin, *The
English Church in the Fourteenth Century* (Cambridge, 1955),
p. 145, says, "Holkot on Wisdom was one of the best-sellers
of the age, the sort of book you would be sure to find in every
respectable late medieval library." The remarks on this story
were incorporated by Berchorius in his commentary on the
Metamorphoses, with a reference to their source. Following
Ovid's account in *Met.* 11.633 ff., Holkot explains, *In librum
sapientiae* (Basel, 1586), pp. 632-634, that there are three dream
messengers: Morpheus, Icelos, and Phantasos. Morpheus appears to the dreamer in human form with human speech and
gesture. Icelos assumes the shapes of beasts and birds, and
Phantasos appears in the forms of inanimate objects. All three
represent types of worldly solicitude. Chaucer's Alcyone is
obviously suffering from solicitude of this kind over the loss
of what is to her a gift of Fortune in human form, and it is
clear that her dream originates within herself. On the other
hand, it was widely held in the fourteenth century, even by
such authorities as Bradwardine, that the substance of dreams
frequently incorporates divine warnings. In Chaucer's poem, the
dream results from solicitude, but the message it contains may
be thought of as Providential, even though Alcyone is unable to
understand it.

[11] For this variety of "sleep" as distinguished from that referred to above in note 4, see Rom. 13.11-13, 1 Cor. 15.34, Eph.
5.14, 1 Thess. 5.4-8. The awakening here urged is sometimes
celebrated in the medieval *aube*.

suggests one darkened by loss of the guiding light of reason. The approach to the cave is a valley between two rocks where nothing grows. The cave is dark as "helle-pit," it contains Lethean streams, and the figures within it are asleep.[12]

Morpheus is awakened rudely by Juno's messenger, who cries " 'Awake,' wonder hie." Morpheus provides that an image of Seys be brought to the dreaming Alcyone. Seys reveals the truth of his condition, and thus of her own, if she will awaken:

> My swete wyf,
> Awake! let be your sorwful lyf!
> For in your sorwe there lyeth no red
> For, certes, swete, I nam but ded. (201-204)

Seys is dead and thus, like Troilus as he ascends through the spheres, beyond illusion and beyond remedy. Thus Seys is able to reveal a truth which would have been available even to pagans like Cicero; but Alcyone, whose mind is darkened by grief, does not respond to her husband's message. Seeing nothing but her temporal loss, she does not hear the wisdom he has to offer.

To the speaker, who knows "phisicien but oon"— "I ne knew never god but oon"—and can thus see in Alcyone's vision the wisdom which she is unable to perceive—"Ne she koude no rede but oon"—the story could suggest a solution to his own difficulties. If he desired the truth and was prepared to heed it, he would be able to receive a vision which would bring the peace of mind he desires. Alcyone received without understanding a message that the speaker would like to find again for himself. Thus he vows to give Mor-

[12] For the streams see the *Ovide moralisé*, 10.258-269.

41

pheus or Juno, or "som wight elles," a bed. The vow
of the bed is elaborately developed. It is to be of dove's
feathers, white within, adorned with gold, and covered
in black satin. More than this, the feather-bed will be
ensconced in a magnificent chamber with surrounding
halls. These rooms will be painted entirely in gold and
adorned with tapestry "of oo sute." Someone up there
takes this vow seriously so that the poet falls asleep
over his book, and dreams a dream.

The poet's splendid offer and its unexpectedly sud-
den soporific result are so happily ludicrous as not to
need comment. On the other hand, the elaborateness of
the vow does open up the possibility of highly appropriate symbolic values which provide another level of
transition from wakefulness to dream. The bed is a
traditional symbol for contemplation; so too are the
feathers, the gold, the black cover, and the pillows.[13]
The rooms which he vows also suggest contemplation.
The manner of their decoration is reminiscent of that
of Solomon's Temple, traditional symbol of the inner
mind adorned to receive the Truth in prayer and contemplation.[14]

[13] The meaning of the bed is fairly obvious. However, see,
for example, Rabanus, *De universo*, *PL*, 111, 79; Peter Lombard
on Ps. 6.6, *PL*, 191, 107. For feathers, see Alanus, *Distinctiones*,
PL, 210, 897. Although gold is usually associated with wisdom,
it may also suggest contemplation; see *ibid*., 714. The black
cover probably suggests outward tribulation or penance. See
Allegoriae, *PL*, 112, 1006. Cf. the epithet "Black Prince"
adopted by Edward of Woodstock. For pillows, see Bede on
Mark 4.38, *PL*, 92, 174. These references do not imply that
Chaucer had specific Scriptural verses in mind as sources for
the details. Rather, the context of the details is so arranged as
to suggest certain commonplace associations.

[14] See Bede, *De templo Salomonis liber*, *PL*, 91, 757-758. For
the gold, see col. 752, and tapestry, col. 770.

If the possibility of such fairly obvious symbolic values is granted, behind the humor of the transitional passage rests a further signification; the poet has responded sufficiently to the story of Seys and Alcyone to recognize that he must order his own mind if he is to find the comfort in his bereavement which the true Physician alone can give. Alanus says, in defining the symbolic sense of a bed, "just as in bed the sick man labors, the healthy man is at peace: so in the conscience the sinner labors, the just man is at peace."[15] On the symbolic level, the transition to the dream suggests that the poet finds sleep because his reading has prepared him to dream dreams purposefully. The transition also suggests that the dream will have a curative effect.

When the speaker has expressed his proper intentions, the contemplation he desires comes to him "sodeynly"; he falls asleep "ryght upon" his book. Chaucer comments that the dream he saw was so "ynly" sweet and so "wonderful" that no one—not even Joseph or Macrobius—could interpret it correctly. The exaggerated surface humor of the preceding passage is maintained, but obviously Chaucer is not saying that there is no use listening to the dream because any attempt at interpretation will be futile. What he does instead is to hint that the wonder and inward sweetness of the dream make it well worth interpreting. The statement is a humorous admonition to go beyond the sense to the doctrine within.

The dream begins (290-293) with a definite indication of time of year, May, and the time of day, dawn. The dreamer is awakened by the singing of birds (294-320), sitting on his "chambre roof" and singing a "solempne servise," that

[15] *PL*, 210, 843.

43

> But hyt had be a thyng of heven—
> So mery a soun, so swete entewnes,
> That certes, for the town of Tewnes
> I nolde but I had herde hem synge. (308-311)

He discovers that his chamber is windowed with painted glass, depicting the "story of Troye," and the walls are "peynted" with "both text and glose of al the Romaunce of the Rose" (321-334). Through the windows the sun is shining. It is a cloudless, temperate day (335-343).

Are these details merely empty "convention," borrowed purely imitatively by Chaucer, or do they have significance? A leading question, for the great poet (our assumption) will not merely dress up conventions; he will use them meaningfully. And what is meaningful in the details which open the dream is not hard to come by, even for the modern reader if he is willing to make use of the obvious.

Most obviously, staying within the poem itself, the beginning of the dream contrasts sharply with the details of the story which put the poet to sleep. The temporal setting of the story of Alcyone is not given, except for the fact that Seys appears to Alcyone in her swoon, "a quarter before day," that is, in the dark or the false dawn in contrast to the poet's awakening in the bright, full dawn of a May day. Other details are contrasted: Morpheus' rocky cave, dark "as helle-pit," filled with "a dedly slepynge sown," the difficult awakening of Morpheus, as against the brightly painted, radiantly lighted room filled with the "solempne servise" of the birds which seemed "a thyng of hevene," and, finally, the poet's pleasant awakening. If the details of the story of Seys and Alcyone had relevant sym-

44

bolic values, so should the contrasting details of the dream.

The transition from story-reading to dreaming is stressed by triple repetition:

> Loo, thus hyt was, thys was my sweven,
> Me thoghte thus: that hyt was May,
> And in the dawenynge I lay
> (Me mette thus) in my bed al naked. (290-293)

Emphasis is thus given to the details of the dream which must not be left unexamined as merely suggestive of Spring or as merely conventional or as providing merely a poetic parallel to the dawn in the Alcyone story. In interpreting the symbols in the dream we must posit its locale as the mind of a poet, darkened by loss, but incipiently lightened if he has understood the story of Seys and Alcyone, that he may sleep and in a dream perhaps hear and heed the message of the one Physician. To put the matter simply, the poet is suffering because Blanche the Duchess has died; his comfort must come from Christ, who died and was resurrected. And the Spring is the season of the Resurrection. In the annual calendar of his memory the Resurrection is a recent event, a reminder of the source of comfort. The dawn, too, is a conventional symbol not only of the Resurrection, but of the *lux divinae cognitionis* in the individual.[16]

The birds, in singing the "solempne servise" which awakens the dreamer, are performing what appears to be a symbolic action. The harmony of the bird's song is a conventional reflection of the heavenly harmony,[17]

[16] *Ibid.*, 770.
[17] *Ibid.*, 1009. Cf. St. Ambrose, *Hexameron*, *PL*, 14, 237-238; Gregory, *Moralia*, *PL*, 76, 97. It may be significant that in

but the "solempne servise" would appear to have specific relevance to the subject of bereavement. The song of heavenly harmony provides an appropriate device for awakening the dreamer to the May dawn and the sun, with its omnipresent symbolic value, perhaps here of the *lux divinae cognitionis.* Suggesting, as it does, the service of Lauds and the Resurrection, the song provides very different awakening from the rude awakening of Morpheus in the unillumined cave.

Whatever one's reluctance to add to the number of Chaucer's puns, here he does appear to play with words in such a way as to enforce the symbolism of "solempne servise":

> So mery a sown, so swete entewnes,
> That certes, for the town of Tewnes
> I nolde but I had herd hem synge. (309-311)

Literally as "town of Tunis," the phrase has no apparent value except to provide a rhyme. But "town of tewnes," allowing for the usual flexibility of vocalic shifting common to word play, may also be read as "tune of tunes," i.e., song of songs, or "Town of Towns," i.e. the New Jerusalem. The Song of Songs is the song of love between Christ and His Church, or between Christ and the soul of the faithful which seeks union with Him in the New Jerusalem. The dreamer's awakening has placed before him the possibility of peace for his unquiet heart. And immediately he notes the sun illuminating his painted windows, with their Aeneid-like story, and lighting the painted walls, with their story and gloss of the *Romaunce of the Rose.*

Bede's account of the Temple of Solomon, *PL*, 91, 751, the roof is made up of *tabulata* on three levels where the three types of faithful in the Church sing in praise of God.

46

The Book of the Duchess

No reader of Dante will need to be reminded that the medieval reader considered that the *Aeneid* was illumined through Christian understanding, which saw in Aeneas' search for the new city the pilgrimage of the human spirit. Similarly in the light of doctrine, the gloss on the *Romaunce of the Rose* would serve as a warning against the idolatry of the lover who enters the garden of amorous delight.[18] "Late, this other night," presumably by candlelight, the poet had read the story of Seys and Alcyone in a collection,

> That clerks had in olde tyme,
> And other poets, put in rime.

Now other stories are presented to him, dreaming, in the light of the sun shining through or illuminating them. Perhaps only coincidentally, but none the less aptly, it was another Aeneas who was cured of his eight years' illness by the one Physician, and in the description of the poet's illness at the beginning of the poem, one possible diagnosis was love-sickness, the illness of the lover of the Rose.

At all events, the sun illumines the bed of the dreamer, as it does the atmosphere outside the room. The air is temperate, and the sky is without any clouds. In the *Miscellanea* attributed in Migne to Hugh of St. Victor is a passage which may help to explain the significance of these details and their relation to the dreamer. Heaven is described as a place of light without

[18] For Chaucer's attitude toward the meaning of the *Roman*, see *LGW*, Prologue (G) 458ff. His use of the poem suggests that his attitude toward it must have resembled that taken later by Pierre Col, rather than that taken by Christine de Pisan and Jean Gerson. Cf. D. W. Robertson, Jr., *A Preface to Chaucer* (Princeton, 1962), pp. 91-104.

clouds, "lux sine nubes." It is filled with the praise of God sung by the bands of the blessed. This Heaven cannot be seen with the eyes, but only through the mind guided by the Church. Perhaps this is why the dreamer can see the sun only as it shines through painted windows or as it is reflected on the painted walls. In his mind alone may the dreamer catch a glimpse of the heaven he may attain by faithful attention to the teachings of the Church.[19] In his dream the poet may find curative peace by seeing the experience of his grief in the light of the truth of God's heaven. It is not enough, however, to contemplate; action is required, and the dreamer is called from his bed.

As Morpheus was aroused by a horn to provide Alcyone with the image of her husband, the dreamer is aroused to activity by hearing a hunting horn blow and the sounds of hunters speaking of hunting the hart, and of how the hart has become "embosed," exhausted. The dreamer declares:

> I was ryght glad, and up anoon
> Took my hors, and forth I wente
> Out of my chambre. (356-358)

He meets with a "route" of hunters and learns from one, leading a dog, that it is "th' emperour Octovyen" who will be hunting. Again the dreamer is pleased.

> "A Goddes half, in good tyme!" quod I,
> "Go we faste!" and gan to ryde. (370-371)

The hunt begins in earnest. The hart is discovered, chased, and then,

> This hert rused, and staal away
> Fro alle the houndes a privy way. (381-382)

The "forloyn" is blown.

[19] Cf. *PL*, 177, 702.

There is in all this, at least on the surface, a dream-like air of inconsequence. When the dreamer hears of the hart it is "embosed," but the hunt begins in earnest later, and only then does the hart steal away. The dreamer apparently mounts his horse inside his chamber.[20] He is utterly unsurprised, but he is delighted first to hear that the hunt has begun and then to hear that the hunter is the "Emperor Octovyen." The symbolic level may provide a consistent meaning for these details.

The exposition of this symbolism may well begin with the double meaning of "hert," *hart* and *heart*, and the commonplace allegorization of God as the Hunter-King hunting after the human soul.[21] In addition, the name of the King, "Octovyen," may contain an etymological pun: *octo*, "eight," and *vyen* "coming." The number *eight* signifies Christ's Resurrection, the recollection of which has already been suggested by the song of the birds in the May dawn, or the resurrection of the faithful on the Day of Judgment. Again, it suggests the kind of inner resurrection implied by the end of the eight years' malady.[22] The mounting of the horse

[20] This inconsequence has been noted, and in one case has seemed sufficiently inexplicable to warrant an unsupported emendation of the text. See Robinson's notes on lines 357-358 and 368.

[21] See Ps. 41.1 and Lombard, *PL*, 191, 415-416. The idea is taken up in Bede's *Soliloquium*, *AH*, 50.114-115. Cf. 3 Kings 4.23, and Rabanus, *PL*, 109, 131. The idea is reflected in *The Bestiary of Guillaume le Clerc*, trans., G. C. Druce (Ashford, Kent, 1936), ll. 2815-2816. See also *Gesta romanorum*, *EETS*, LXIX, p. 320.

[22] On "eight," see Rabanus, *De universo*, *PL*, 111, 491; Bede, *De templo Salomonis*, *PL*, 91, 806; Gregory, *PL*, 76, 1341, 1391;

49

may be used to suggest the proper intention of the dreamer.[23] The apparent inconsequence of the "embosed" hart, for whom the hunt begins in earnest only after the dreamer joins the hunt, but who later escapes, has relation to the two states of mind of the dreaming poet. On the one hand, he is a "mased" creature like Alcyone, insensible to comfort; the "hart" who steals away is like the heart of the poet, too overcome by grief to heed the message of wisdom. On the other hand, the poet, because he is aware of the Physician who can cure his malady, vaguely realizes the solution to his problem. There are, as it were, two parts of the poet's mind, one grieving at the loss of what appears to have been a gift of Fortune, and another aware of the sources of rational consolation. Medieval readers were familiar with inner divisions of this kind, most obviously, perhaps, in the *Consolation* of Boethius, where, as glosses like Trivet's explained, a dialogue takes place between two aspects of a single person, one wise and knowing, the other confused by the whims of Lady Fortune. We should understand that inner divisions of this kind in medieval texts are not aspects of "psychology" in the modern sense, but of moral philosophy.

Lombard, introduction to Ps. 6, *PL*, 191, 103. Cf. the meaning of the octave in St. Augustine, *De trinitate*, 4.3, and, for some notion of the pervasiveness of the idea, Richard Krautheimer, "Introduction to an 'Iconography of Mediaeval Architecture.'" *JWCI*, v (1942), p. 11. The Resurrection was celebrated on the eighth day (Sunday), and late medieval baptismal fonts commonly had eight sides to suggest the resurrection of the baptized Christian with Christ. See Berchorius, *Reductorium morale*, Book XIII, xxviii, "octonarius signat beatitudinem et tempus future resurrectionis." Cf. Robertson, *Preface*, pp. 122-124.

[23] For the horse and horn see Alanus, *Distinctiones*, *PL*, 210, 780 and 949.

This division in the mind of the dreamer may suggest an important clue to the meaning of the ensuing
action. Suddenly, after he hears the "forloyn," the
dreamer says,

> I was go walked fro my tree,
> And as I wente, ther cam by mee
> A whelp, that fauned me as I stood,
> That hadde yfolowed, and koude no good.
>
> (387-390)

He, in turn, follows the whelp along a flowery path
in a shady wood, until he comes to a "man in blak"
with his back to an old oak tree. The remainder of the
dream reports the conversation between the dreamer,
who had left his tree, and the grieving Black Knight,
who is found leaning against a tree. The Black Knight
is commonly identified as John of Gaunt, but beyond
the reasonable assurance that the poem is about his
deceased Duchess, there is little basis for this identification, which has not gone unchallenged. There are
reasons to distrust it. The Black Knight's age is given
very specifically as twenty-four; John was twenty-nine
when Blanche died—a small discrepancy, but the argument for the identification must take it into account.
There is no evidence to suggest—as with Richard II
—any extravagant grief over the loss of his wife; indeed he remarried very soon, although for purely po-
litical reasons. This fact supplies no evidence either
way, but does raise the question of whether Chaucer
was writing to console the Duke or to eulogize the
Duchess, two matters not necessarily the same. At any
event, would not Chaucer in picturing the Alcyone-like
violence of the Black Knight's grief have been treading
on potentially tactless ground? Would the Duke have

been flattered? Further, the line of description, "upon hys berd but lytel her" (456), seems hardly designed to flatter. John may not have been vain, or, at best, vain about his beard. But the beard was considered the "ornament of a man's face," and a sign of masculinity.[24] To say that John's beard had "little hair" would hardly have been tactful. Finally, how pleased might John have been with Chaucer's picture of himself as the Black Knight under the tutelage of Blanche, so that, in effect, he overcame his youthful folly through her?

Such arguments as these have convinced us that the Black Knight was not intended as the dream representative of John of Gaunt, but rather as a sorrowing alter ego of the speaker in the poem, like the poet himself representative of all those who have honored and loved Blanche and lost her in death. However, the biographical question is not central to our reading of the dream dialogue. We find it more consonant with what is in the poem and with historical probability to assume that the Black Knight is not John of Gaunt. For us the importance of the Black Knight in the poem rests in the fact of his being Alcyone-like in his grief. He *is*, in effect, grief itself. Whether the dreamer learns the nature of his own sorrow from observing a simulacrum or the dream representative of an historical person is not too material; those who feel strongly that the Black Knight is John of Gaunt can replace the general with the particular. For them the dreamer will discover the

[24] Berchorius, *Reductorium morale*, II, xiii. Berchorius cites Chaucer's "daun Constantyn." He equates the beard with virtue, and states that three types of persons are lacking in beards, women, *castrati* and boys, types of the effeminate, those cut off from virtue, and the ignorant. See also Alanus, *PL*, 210, 826.

truth of his own sorrow through observation of John's grief; for us he discovers the truth in an alter ego, representative of his own grief. In what follows we assume that the Black Knight is *not* John of Gaunt.

The situation in the dream very possibly suggests the story which inspired the poet to dream in the first place. At the heart of his dream he finds a "mased" Alcyone-like person. Just as Seys came to Alcyone, so he as a rational being confronts a creature like that part of him which is immersed in irrational grief because of an act of Fortune. Here is the significance of the dreamer leaving his tree to find the Knight in mourning leaning against a tree.[25] In effect, the point is a fairly simple one, however devious the allegorical vehicle may seem to be. Grace is available to man, but only if he prepares himself to receive it. The sorrowing poet must search his own heart for understanding, and this is the "hunt" with which the remainder of the poem is concerned. The loss of Blanche must be seen not as a loss of a gift of Fortune but as an inspiration. It is important, moreover, not that the dreamer specifically be led to see this, but that the audience of the poem be led to understand it. The subject of the poem is not the poet, but the Duchess whom it eulogizes.

The details of the poet's discovery of his mourning self through facing its simulacrum are perhaps symbolic. The whelp, for example, may have a fairly specific significance in relation to the hounds from whom the hart had stolen away. In the symbolism of the hunt, the hounds have a traditional role as preachers. But the

[25] If other precedents are wanted in addition to the *De consolatione* for the kind of inner dialogue suggested here, cf. St. Augustine's *Soliloquium*, Dante's *Vita nuova*, or Petrarch's *Secretum*.

hart has escaped the hounds, and it is the whelp, who could not thrive in the hunt, who leads the dreamer to the vision of his "mased" inner self. What is intended here is perhaps suggested by the symbolic distinction between dogs and whelps in the *De bestiis et aliis rebus*, a commonplace book. After discussing the various functions of hounds, the author describes the curative functions of hounds and whelps considered symbolically as priests. Hounds with their tongues represent priests who heal sins which are revealed at confession. Whelps represent priests in their function of curing both by word and by example sins unwittingly retained in the mind and thus not confessed.[26] The cure "in opere vel sermone" is much the same as that which succeeded with Aeneas after his eight years' malady.[27] The poet, as he is pictured at the beginning of the poem, is unrepentant, but the words and examples of those who seek to console him nevertheless bring him to a realization that only a part of him is lost.

The hart, as we recall, escaped the hounds "a privy way," which may imply that he separated himself from his fellows by retiring into his private sorrows where no external ministrations could reach him. To help him find himself, the whelp leads the dreamer down a flowery path through the woods.[28] The grove is so flowery

[26] That the whelp "koude no good" (390) suggests in context his wordless, humble role of teaching by example rather than by preaching. Further, the hart is symbolically complex. The "defaute" (389) of the hunters does not represent their inability but the lost state of the mourner. The whelp, too, may reflect this state.

[27] See above, note 3.

[28] One of the traditional meanings of *semita* is *cogitatio*. See Alanus, *Distinctiones*, PL, 210, 940. The "privy" way suggests solitude which, *ibid.*, 948, may represent "separatio ab Ecclesia." Cf. *Gregorianum*, PL, 193, 269-270.

that the earth seemed to wish to be "gayer than the heven." It is a typical earthly paradise whose delights are transitory. The branches shade the grass and flowers so as to form a sort of "via tenebrosa" whose shadows indicate oblivion. Finally the dreamer finds an image of his grief-stricken self in the black of tribulation, leaning against an oak, the tree of despair, perhaps the same symbolic tree from which he in rationality had walked.[29]

Whatever the meaning of the whelp, the dreamer has walked from his tree, through a wooded path, to find his own suffering, but now viewed in another person. In his grief the poet had lost sight of the only source of comfort, God. The true reason for his sorrow is error; the speaker had been temporarily misled to believe that the loss of another human was the cause of his grief. In Christian fact there can be no sorrow except that arising in separation from God. A man's love has two sides, one false (cupidity) the other true (charity); his grief has two sides, one *tristitia*, false grief caused by the loss of an object of desire, the other a true grief caused by his enforced bodily separation from God. What the speaker had taken as grief was itself false worldly vanity. It is to understand this that the dreamer, representing the released rationality of the poet, is led to view in another person the false sorrow into which he had chosen to fall. Therefore, the recognition of the man in black by the dreamer is not immediate, but follows only, as it were, his awakening to the realization of the sober truth about himself.

[29] The scenery in general resembles that of the garden of Deduit in the *Roman de la rose*. For the blackness of the knight and the oak, see *Allegoriae*, PL, 112, 1006, 1036. Cf. the oak under which Delyt stands alone in *The Parliament of Fowls*, discussed below, Ch. III.

As he approaches, the dreamer sees that the man in black seems by his manner to be "A wonder wel-farynge knyght." The knightly status need not be either literally autobiographical or indicative of "historical allegory." All Christians became knights spiritually at Confirmation. Symbolically all who live are in battle either as knights of God or as knights of the world.[30] His age of twenty-four may have an incidental symbolic value. It would place the Black Knight in the period of adolescence, which extended from fourteen to twenty-eight. It is the period when man should be informed by precepts and ruled by counsel, so that he may learn to conquer himself.[31]

The dreamer takes up a position behind the Black Knight and hears him complain piteously:

> Hit was gret wonder that Nature
> Myght suffre any creature
> To have such sorwe, and be not ded. (467-468)

In this detail and in the subsequent description of the Knight's condition, it becomes clear that he is exactly in the same situation as the speaker at the beginning of the poem whose mode of life was "ageynes kynde." In contrast to the song of the birds, which had reminded the dreamer of the "toun of Tewnes," the song of the Black Knight is "withoute noote, withoute song." The song that the birds sang was one of joy in God. The Black Knight's song is without melodious joy; it is a song of sorrow for an earthly object.[32] The song itself states explicitly the desperate sorrow of the poet's

[30] Gregory, *Moralia, PL*, 76, 618, 1079.

[31] On adolescence, see above, Ch. I, note 19.

[32] A "song without song" is probably one that does not reflect celestial harmony. Cf. Ch. III, note 5, below.

heart. He will never be joyful again because his lady is dead and gone from him. She is good beyond compare. He should himself have died because only his lady can bring him joy. When the Knight has finished his song, the blood rushes to his heart, where the internal wound lies. He falls into a state parallel with that described in the opening lines of the poem. He is oblivious to outward circumstances, wonders how he may live, and lapses into a state contrary to Nature.

Finally the Knight sees the dreamer, and the two exchange courtesies, during which the Knight impresses the dreamer as being strikingly amiable. He spoke

> As hyt had be another wyght. (530)

Perhaps this line means that the Knight is pleasant in spite of his sorrow. He acts like any other man, even though he seems bound in despair. At all events, he is "tretable" even in sorrow. At this point the dreamer has observed the Black Knight closely and overheard his joyless song. He has all the facts at hand to recognize his despair. The questions which he asks, as Professor Kittredge observed, cannot be asked in ignorance but must be part of a deliberate plan. This attitude is supported by the dreamer's statement,

> I gan fynde a tale
> To hym, to loke wher I myght ought
> Have more knowynge of hys thought. (536-538)

By causing the alter ego of his grieving self to make a sort of confession, the dreamer, symbolizing the poet's own rational self, may indicate the way to the solace of truth to the poet, or at least to the reader. The Knight is unconcerned that the hart has escaped:

> Y do no fors therof, quod he;
> My thought ys theron never a del.

57

By oure Lord, quod I, y trow yow wel;
Ryght so me thinketh by youre chere. (542-545)

If the hunt for the hart is significant, then the Knight's statement is indicative of his despairing state. The dreamer promises that if the Black Knight will tell his woe to him, he may be able to amend it. But the despairing one is unable to believe in this possibility of comfort:

No man may my sorwe glade,
That maketh my hewe to falle and fade,
And hath myn understondynge lorn,
That me ys wo that I was born! (563-566)

The sorrow upon which he is wilfully fixed has deprived him of understanding, which the intellect alone can supply. He demonstrates that he has lost his understanding in his list of impossible cures. Ovid cannot cure him of his love. Orpheus with his melody may not raise his spirits. Dedalus with his magic may not divert him. The speaker at the beginning of the poem knows that there is one Physician who may cure him, but the despairing Black Knight feels that there is no cure because the lady has died. When he speaks of the impossibility of any physician curing him, he refers to the founders of medicine:

Ne hele me may no phisicien,
Noght Ypocras ne Galyen.
Me ys wo that I lyve houres twelve. (571-573)

Because his lady has died, it is painful to him even that he must live for twelve hours. But in rejecting the twelve hours, perhaps the Knight inadvertently reveals the cause of his sorrow. There are twelve hours in the day, and he who walks in the day walks under the pro-

tection of the Physician.[33] His complete abandonment
to sorrow is also indicated in his unavailing desire for
death and his considerable self-pity. His pains are
greater than those of "Cesiphus"; indeed, he exclaims,

For y am sorwe and sorwe ys y. (597)

Sisyphus was a thief whose futile task was thought to
represent, not, as some would now have it, the Fate of
Man, but the punishment of those who persist in their
iniquity.[34] If the Knight's sorrow is, as he says, greater
than that of Sisyphus, he has indeed created for himself
a Hades of *tristitia*.

The Knight's worldly virtues and comforts, as he
explains at some length, have become vices and dis-
comforts. As a result, among other things, he is sorrowful, idle, wrathful, ill, fearful, foolish, wakeful,
and at strife. This change from his apparently happy
former state he attributes to the hypocritical falseness of
Fortune, the idol of false portraiture, as he calls her.
She promises all, but keeps no promise. She seems to
walk upright in integrity, but actually she is halt. She
seems fair, but is inwardly foul, and so on. There is a
direct relation between the doubleness of Fortune and
the abrupt change in all that has been dear to him.

[33] John 11.9. Cf. Bruno Astensis, *PL*, 165, 541-542: "Si quis
autem hunc diem sequatur, si quis in eo ambulaverit, si quis
mihi crediderit, non offendet. Cur? *Quia lucem huius mundi
videt. Ego sum lux mundi. Si vero in nocte ambulaverit*, si
errorem et tenebrarum principem secutus fuerit (hoc est enim
in nocte ambulare), offendet et cadet. Cur? *Quia lux non est
in eo*."

[34] G. H. Bode, *Scriptores rerum mythicarum* (Cellis, 1834),
p. 177. This work, attributed variously to Alexander Neckam
and Albericus of London, was extremely popular. Petrarch had
a copy made for his library.

Actually, he has been defeated by Fortune because he has relied on her in too great love for one of her gifts, so that his life partakes of the instability of Fortune. His complaint against false Fortune is another indication of his blindness. Not Fortune but he himself is at fault, for he has relied upon her completely.[35] Figuratively, the Knight ventured to play chess with her in setting his love on things subject to Fortune. The figure is itself a delusion because it implies that a man may win in a game with Fortune. If he had known the truth, the Knight would have realized that when Fortune took his "fers" she was acting in accordance with her nature. His virtues and comforts were dependent on Fortune's external well-seeming. When her true nature becomes apparent, he loses the object of his love, and his comforts and virtues vanish.

The figure of the chess game is used to emphasize the element of Fortune in the Knight's loss and his own lack of reason. It is based on the account of Fortune given by Reason in *The Romance of the Rose*, where King Manfred of Sicily, flaunting the Church, subjects himself to Fortune but is mated by a "paonet errant," losing his "fierce" on the first day of battle. Having told this story, Reason admonishes:

> Veiz ci genz qui granz eneurs tindrent,
> Or sez a quel chief il en vindrent:
> N'est donc bien Fortune seüre;
> N'est bien fos qui s'i asseüre,
> Quant ceus qu'el veaut par devant oindre
> Seaut ainsinc par darriere poindre?
> E tu, qui la rose baisas,
> Par quei de deul si grant fais as

[35] See Boethius, *De cons.*, 2, Pr. 1.

Que tu ne t'en sez apaisier,
Cuidaies tu toujourz baisier,
Toujourz aveir aise e delices?
Par mon chief, tu iés fos e nices. (6741-6752)

The Black Knight had unreasonably expected to maintain "aise e delices," a wish, like Manfred's proud ambition, "Contre la fei de sainte iglise." The only way that he conceives to contend with Fortune is to be more skillful at the "jeupardies," or problems of the game. He is aware that hope of overcoming Fortune by skill is deceiving, but he does not really understand why, except in terms of his blind adoration for his lost lady. He says that if he had been in Fortune's place, or if he had been God who controls Fortune, he would have taken the Queen too, because of her great worth. The Black Knight sees that there is a power which governs Fortune, but he does not see that only by trusting in this power may he triumph over Fortune. In short, the chess game reveals the Black Knight as one who believes in God but must be shown that he must turn to God for comfort.

The contrast between the Black Knight and the dreamer is made explicit. The latter not only knows his Physician but knows also that his Physician may easily be approached, since He is seeking him. Morally, the situation is uniquely that of the will and the intellect. The will must be guided in its love by the knowledge furnished it by the intellect. Not seeing beyond Fortune, the self-willed Knight is reduced to desperation. Since he has lost his bliss, he has no recourse but to end his life:

But through that draughte I have lorn
My blysse—allas! that I was born!—

61

For evermore y trowe trewely;
For al my wille, my lust holly
Ys turned; but yet, what to doone?
Be oure Lord, hyt ys to deye soone. (685-690)

What follows is an explanation from the Black Knight's
point of view of why death is the only recourse for him.
He is determined not to abandon his sorrow over the
loss of his lady. Since he lives for the lady, he must
either find her or die. He looks to the sky and the earth,
but cannot find her, so that the world brings him only
weeping. But his sorrow brings him nothing; that is, he
owes it nothing for anything gained from it. No gladness may refresh him, and he has lost the sufficiency
that makes life possible. Thus only death is left. Like
Tantalus (709), who, as Trivet explains in his commentary on Boethius, was too avaricious to supply himself with necessities,[36] the Knight is too much concerned
for his loss to take any care for his own needs.

When the dreamer hears the lament of the Knight, he
remarks,

Unnethe myght y lenger dwelle,
Hyt dyde myn herte so moche woo. (712-713)

The woe of his own "heart," the rused "hart" of Christ's
hunt, is almost unbearable to him. Intellectually, he
strives to correct the false basis of the Black Knight's
despair, asking the Knight to pity his "nature" that
formed him "to creature." This request suggests that
the Image of God, in which he is made, is distorted in
the idolatry of the will.[37] He reminds the Knight of
Socrates, who cared nothing for Fortune, just as Reason

[36] London, British Museum MS Burney 131, fol. 49 verso.
[37] See our *"Piers Plowman" and Scriptural Tradition* (Princeton, 1951), pp. 107-109.

in *The Romance of the Rose* reminded the dreamer of
the same example.[38] This the Knight refuses to heed.

The Black Knight blinds himself to the truth, in part
by means of the simile of the chess game. The dreamer
is aware of this self-deception and knows that the truth
must be acknowledged plainly if the cure for sorrow is
to be effective. He takes up the figure that the Black
Knight has suggested, but in such a way as to indicate
that he understands it figuratively. Literally, there is
only one "fers"; yet the dreamer says that even if the
Black Knight had lost the "ferses twelve," he would not
be justified in committing suicide. Actually, since he has
overheard the Black Knight's opening complaint, the
dreamer knows that he is elegantly alluding to his lady
in the figure of the "fers." But he knows that the plain
statement of the loss must preface the acknowledg-
ment, to paraphrase Seys, that in

> sorwe there lyth no red
> For, certes . . . [she is] but ded.

The Black Knight had said only "I have lorn my
blysse." For his own purposes the dreamer accepts this
statement, later saying,

> Good sir, telle me al hooly
> In what wyse, how, why, and wherfore
> That ye have thus youre blysse lore. (746-748)

By the loss of the "fers" the dreamer pretends to understand the only loss acknowledged by the Knight, the
loss of his bliss.[39] The dreamer now demolishes the

[38] *RR*, 5847-5856. It is significant that Reason in the *Roman*
and the dreamer in Chaucer's poem play very similar parts.
The lines are from the same discourse on Fortune which suggested the figure of the chess game.

[39] Note that "bliss" may have a double meaning: the Knight's

Black Knight's argument that the only course open to him is suicide. First of all, he shows that the amount of the loss has no bearing on the issue, for even if the Black Knight had lost not only bliss but the other fruits of the spirit as well, and had committed suicide, he would be as guilty of homicide as was Medea; for Phyllis, Dido, and Echo, who had committed suicide or died in sorrow, were like Medea, damned for the folly they had done because of earthly grief. The four women also have in common a self-deception caused by idolatry of a gift of Fortune. His last illustration is Samson:

> And for Dalida died Sampson,
> That slough hymself with a piler. (738-739)

Samson's death, however, is significantly different from the others since he did not die "for Dalida," at least in the context of the dreamer's examples. Rather he died in sorrow for his sins, obedient to God's purpose. Moreover, his death was universally taken as prefiguring Christ's sacrifice on the cross. The other suicides are wickedly idolatrous; Samson's death is one of self-sacrifice, of repentance, following God's wishes:[40]

> But ther is no man alyve her
> Wolde for a fers make this woo! (740-741)

Samson, prefiguring the Redeemer, may be said to have

---

false view of it, and the true. Peter Lombard, *PL*, 192, 160, explains *gaudium* as "puritas conscientiae et elatio animi super his quae digna sunt exsultationis." According to Alanus, *PL*, 210, 138-139, *gaudium* frees the mind of care. It is like the garden of Paradise and is a sure protection against the whims of Fortune. Again, it is like the Temple of Solomon.

[40] For Samson as a figure of Christ, see *Glossa ordinaria*, *PL*, 113, 532. The idea is, of course, a commonplace in medieval art.

given his life for a "fers," the supreme act of charity, but no man may throw away his life because he has made his earthly good another human creature.

But the Black Knight does not understand why he should not lament over the loss of an earthly object, and he does not learn the lesson which the dreamer implies. Rather, he continues in his belief that the greatness of his loss is sufficient reason for his unnatural grief:

> Thou wost ful lytel what thou menest;
> I have lost more than thow wenest. (743-744)

These lines become something of a refrain for the remainder of the dialogue as the dreamer, through pretended misunderstanding, draws the Knight into a full confession. The dreamer knows that the Black Knight has lost an earthly object of surpassing worth, but the Black Knight believes that he has lost more than he actually has, for he fails to see his loss in the light of God's Providence. Acknowledging its loss and accepting it as coming from God is the end to which the will must be directed. The dreamer now asks the Black Knight the circumstances of his loss of bliss. The terms of his question are those of the confessional, suggesting that the succeeding dialogue will take the form of a confession in which the true state of the Black Knight will be revealed. Specifically, the dreamer asks two of the traditional circumstantial questions: How? and Why?[41] Before beginning his confession of love, the

[41] For the "circumstances," see *Parson's Tale*, pp. 309-310. For Chaucer's use of confession as a symbolic device in a secular poem, W. A. Pantin's comment on Gower's *Confessio amantis* is to the point, *op.cit.*, p. 227: "Here we have in fact an elegant, moral parody of the contemporary treatises on confession. At first sign it sounds like a piece of profanity, but it is simply an

Black Knight has the dreamer swear to listen atten-
tively. The swearing of the oath is humorously formal,
indicative of his patient willingness to hear out the
Black Knight. The Knight in being so earnestly insist-
ent that the dreamer realize the seriousness of the situation appears from the outset a little ridiculous. He demands

> That thou shalt hooly, with al thy wyt,
> Doo thyn entent to herkene hit. (751-752)

When we remember that the Knight is simply asking
the dreamer to be attentive, his pertinacious solemnity
seems humorously childish, and witless. The simple reply of the dreamer, "Yis, syr," dissatisfies him. "Swere
thy trouthe therto," he insists. "Gladly," replies the
dreamer, but this is not enough for the Knight: "Do
thanne holde therto." Patiently, the dreamer makes
his formal vow:

> I shal ryght blythely, so God me save,
> Hooly, with al the wit I have,
> Here you, as wel as I kan. (755-757)

Except for one important detail the dreamer's vow recalls that which Alcyone made to Juno:

> And hooly youres becom I shal
> With goode wille, body, herte, and al. (115-116)

The contrast is that the dreamer's vow significantly involves only his wit. The roles played by the Knight and
the dreamer in their dialogue seem to be those of will

---

example of the medieval love of allegory; men were as ready
to make moral allegory out of the technique of confession as
they were to make a moral allegory out of Noah's Ark or Ovid's
Metamorphoses."

and wit, roles suggested not only by the contrast between the wording of the dreamer's vow and that of
Alcyone, but more strongly by the Knight's self-re-
ported vow to love, which is almost identical with that
of Alcyone. He vowed to Love that he would

> hooly with good entente
> And through plesaunce become his thral
> With good wille, body, hert, and al. (766-768)

A parallel between the Knight and Alcyone is suggested, as well as their difference from the dreamer.
As they are associated with the will, he is associated
with the wit.

The confession begins with due solemnity, "A Goddes half." For the Black Knight, however, what ensues
is not a confession but an act of self-justification for the
extremity of his grief. His basic position is that the
greatness of his loss excuses the greatness of his sorrow.
He explains why he was susceptible to such a great loss,
disclaiming in this way any responsibility. First he explains that it was "kyndely" understanding and his
"owne wyt" that led him to do homage to love,

> That hyt plesance to hym were,
> And worship to my lady dere. (773-774)

However, at the time he made the vow to serve his
lady, he had not met her.

> And this was longe, and many a yer,
> Or that myn herte was set owher,
> That I dide thus, and nyste why;
> I trowe hit cam me kyndely. (775-778)

The Knight seems to say that he has the will's natural
propensity to love so that his service to love was in accord with nature and thus justified. What is more, he

continues, offering still another explanation, his mind when he came to love was "as a whit wal or a table" (780) prepared to receive any kind of impression. Any impressions he received were not his responsibility; his thought, or wit, put love there. Since love was there first, he chose it, and since he chose it first, it has been there ever since. This happened before too much knowledge had turned his heart to malice, which stands in opposition to love. As a final explanation, he says that love came to him in early youth when man is naturally idle and when his thoughts are uncontrolled.[42]

On the surface, these hasty and inconsistent explanations, however typical of the earthly lover, are not reasonable. Considered on the level of *sentence* they involve an unwitting confession of lost innocence, but not a very good confession. The Knight's sorrow is not the sorrow of true repentance,[43] but sorrow arising directly from his error. Moreover, he disavows responsibility, thus repeating the sin of Adam in blaming Eve for his fall.[44] Specifically, he blames his wit for his own wilful irrationality in paying homage to Love as the abstract of his desire. He blames nature, saying that his tendency to earthly love came to him "kyndely." This was evidently a favorite device. A typical warning against it in a standard handbook of penance runs: "He [the penitent] should know the sin to be his own, nor should he wish to excuse himself lest he make his crime greater, as Adam did."[45] The "white table" he mentions is a symbol of innocence, so that the description of its dedication to earthly love is an unwitting description of lost

[42] On *pueritia*, see above, Ch. I, note 19.
[43] On true contrition, see *Parson's Tale*, p. 310.
[44] Cf. St. Augustine, Sermo xx, *PL*, 38, 139.
[45] *De vera et falsa poenitentia*, *PL*, 40, 1126.

innocence.[46] In youth he was governed by idleness, the sin which leads to cupidity; his works were not the works of charity, but "flyttynge"; and everything was "ylyche good" to him. He was thus exactly in the same confused condition as Alcyone or as the speaker at the beginning of the poem. It is a condition which he should long since have overcome, since the age of adolescence is one in which one subjects oneself to discipline, is informed by precept, and is ruled by counsel.[47] In short, the Knight reveals that through wilfulness he has lost his innocence in youth because he was governed by idleness.

Continuing his apologia, the Knight tells of his first encounter with his lady. He was introduced to a fair company, not by "hap or grace," but by Fortune, "false trayteresse pervers" (813). Among the ladies in the company, one was much fairer than the others, excelling them in beauty, in manner, and in every way. The Knight was caught so suddenly that he took "no maner counseyl but at hir lok" and at his own heart (840-841). Fortune, as Boethius shows, has control under God only over that which happens externally to man. It has no control over his heart unless he wills his service to Fortune by loving too much one of its gifts and thus abandoning reason. To complain of Fortune is thus irrational; it is a false way of shifting responsibility. He complains of Fortune,

> For now she worcheth me ful woo. (813)

[46] The table, like most of the other details in this passage, is from Machaut's *Remede de Fortune*. Lines 26-28 (ed. Hoeppfner) read, "Car le droit estat d'innocence / Ressamble proprement la table / Blanche...." Innocence is necessary for a place in the New Jerusalem.

[47] See above, Ch. I, note 19.

Fortune is appointed by God as a trial to the just in prosperity and grief, leading man to turn from God either in the delights of the world or in the world's adversity. The Black Knight has succumbed to both temptations, as his complaint against Fortune reveals. In admitting that it was in answer to his plea that Love brought the lady into his thought and that he took counsel only at her look and at his heart, the Knight implies that the wit was responsible:

> That purely tho myn owne thoght
> Seyde hit were beter serve hir for noght
> Than with another to be wel. (843-845)

He irrationally shifts the blame to wit in the very act of disregarding wit. Actually, as we begin to discover, both Fortune and wit have benefited the will, revealing to him a lady so virtuous that through her example he is led into good action. In the description that follows, we are shown how the lady leads him to virtuous love through the love of her virtues. She brings him out of his wilful childishness and governs him in his first youth. Like Dante's Beatrice, she serves as a model and guide.

As we shall see, in the description of the lady, the details are contrived so as to suggest not only the beauty of the flesh which the Knight sees, but also the true beauty of the spirit. Her beauty is like that of the sun; she surpasses others in beauty as the sun surpasses the moon or the seven stars. That is, she surpasses others as Christ surpasses the church and the saints and yields them the brightness of his own light. Rabanus gives the key to the comparison: "For the sun expresses the idea of the Savior in that just as it exceeds the other sidereal bodies, that is, the moon and the stars, in bril-

liance . . . so also Christ, radiant with His own virtue
and needing assistance from no one, lends the radiance
of virtue and wisdom to holy Church and to its saints."[48]
The luminosity here suggested is also the light of charity, which is most intense in Christ. This light may
radiate from the human heart throughout the whole
body, producing an incomparable beauty. St. Bernard's
account of this process suggests several of the features
of the Black Knight's description:

"But when the splendor of that charity fills the
depths of the heart more abundantly, it is necessary that
it shine forth without, like a light hidden under a bushel
[cf. Mark 4. 21-22, Luke 8. 16-17], or, more appropriately, like a light which shines in the darkness and
does not know how to be hidden [cf. John 1. 5]. Then
the body, the image of the mind, receives it shining
and throwing forth its rays, and diffuses it through its
members and senses, until it appears in its actions, its
words, its looks, its gait, its laughter (if there is laughter) mingled with gravity and full of dignity. Then
when the movements, actions, and functions of the
members and senses are grave, pure, modest, free from
all insolence and effrontery, foreign to both levity and
listlessness, but disposed in equity and devoted to piety,
the beauty of the soul will become manifest, provided
that no hypocrisy lurks within it. For these things may
all be simulated and may not be derived from an over-
flowing heart. And that this beauty of the spirit may
be understood more clearly, that virtue in which we
find it may perhaps be defined: it is that noble demeanor
of the mind solicitous to preserve with a good conscience the integrity of reputation. Or, according to the
Apostle [2 Cor. 8. 21], *we forecast what may be good*

[48] *De universo, PL*, 111, 268.

not only before God, but also before men. Blessed is
the spirit which invests itself with that chaste beauty,
as if with the whiteness of celestial innocence through
which it achieves for itself a glorious conformity not
with the world but with the Word, whence it is said
that it is [Wisdom 7. 26] *the brightness* [candor] *of
eternal life,* and [Heb. 1. 3] *the brightness of his glory
and the figure of his substance.*"[49]

The lady's serious yet joyful demeanor, her radiance,
her "whiteness," all arise from charity. The white radiance of Blanche is a reflection and a promise of the
white radiance of the celestial city.

The theme of the description of the lady is set in the
opening lines:

> I sawgh hyr daunce so comlily,
> Carole and synge so swetely,
> Laughe and pleye so womanly,
> And loke so debonairly,
> So goodly speke and so frendly,
> That, certes, y trowe that evermor
> Nas seyn so blysful a tresor.
> For every heer on hir hed,
> Soth to seyne, hyt was not red,
> Ne nouther yelowe, ne broun hyt nas,
> Me thoghte most lyk gold hyt was. (848-858)

These attractions serve as a summary of the lady's beauty, in act and word. The attributes of singing and dancing on the level of sense are social graces appropriately
put first on the list of those things which attracted the
Black Knight to the lady. If these actions are truly

[49] *Sermones in cantica, PL,* 183, 1193, or *Opera* (Rome, 1957
ff.), II, pp. 314-315. Cf. E. de Bruyne, *Etudes d'esthétique
médiévale* (Bruges, 1946), I, p. 9.

beautiful by medieval standards, they are performed in the worship of God, the source of all beauty.[50] Otherwise they are delusory and false. Singing, as we have suggested, is a typical expression of man's highest activity, praise of God. Beautiful dancing signifies the devotion of a generous heart manifested in good works. Her laughter and play express her spiritual joy. Her eyes, the light of the body, reveal her charitable intention, and her speech is the "goodly" and "friendly" speech of faith. These virtues are crowned by her golden hair, symbolic of the beauty of the virtues in the faithful soul.[51] In these terms the lady is a treasure which thieves may not steal nor moths corrupt, since her virtues are above Fortune. At the very opening of his description, therefore, the Knight indicates the true remedy for his own sorrow. He has been lamenting over the loss of a physical being, although the virtues which inspire his love are not subject to earthly corruption. He

[50] Cf. Peter of Blois, *De amicitia Christiana*, ed. Davy (Paris, 1932), p. 146.

[51] For singing, see Gregory, *Hom. in Ezech.*, PL, 76, 885, or *Allegoriae*, PL, 112, 887. The significance of dancing is explained by Bede on Luke 7.32, PL, 92, 422, and by St. Bonaventura, *Opera* (Quaracchi, 1895), VII, p. 181. Singing and dancing are popular themes in fourteenth-century art. For an example, see the Bohun Psalter in the Nationalbibliothek at Vienna (Cod. 1826*), fol. 85 verso, where Moses and his followers sing and dance after crossing the Red Sea. Cf. Robertson, *Preface*, pp. 130-132, and Fig. 37. On laughter, see *Allegoriae*, PL, 112, 1040 or Alanus, *Anticlaudianus*, PL, 210, 551. Rabanus explains, *De universo*, PL, 111, 149, that the eyes indicate the intention of the heart. For the hair, see *ibid.*, 145. The details in the description show no indication of being "realistic" reflections of the appearance and demeanor of the Duchess of Lancaster. They are, rather, conventional figurative devices designed to indicate her character.

must realize this fact if he is to be cured. The remainder of the description, to the dreamer's first interruption, is concerned with the development of detail.

The lady's eyes, expressing the intention of her heart, are not only gentle and good; they are also "glade and sadde." Although the last two attributes seem to be contradictory, they do not appear so when one considers that the joy is the joy of charity and the seriousness is the seriousness of charitable purpose. Her eyes are also "symple," or without hypocrisy,[52] of great good, and not too wide or staring. Not as in the description of Envy in *The Romance of the Rose*, or commonly in the visual arts, with eyes looking aside, the lady Blanche looked directly, "not asyde ne overthwert," at the object of her attention, seeing it wholly and steadily. The impression of her eyes, because of the charity they expressed, was that "anon she wolde have mercy." Fools, seeing her as an object of desire, mistook this look for what in *The Romance of the Rose* is called "franchise," the generosity of the submissive coquette. But the temperateness of her glance, expressive of temperance within, was completely natural. She never feigned a foolish interest in anyone, even in play. In spite of his understanding of the virtue revealed in the lady's eyes, the Knight, pledged to the God of Love, saw the mercy that fools thought they saw:

> But ever, me thoght, hir eyen seyde,
> Be God, my wrathe ys al foryive! (876-877)

Her eyes reveal the spiritual joy which illumines her so

[52] Cf. Gilbert de Hoyland, *Sermones in Canticum*, PL, 184, 114-115: "Prudenter quidem, quoniam si simplex oculus fuerit, totum corpus lucidum erit. . . . Bona enim est oculata simplicitas, ita simulationem excludens, ut non caliget in veritate."

that "dulnesse was of hir adrad" (879). With spiritual wisdom, *sapientia*, she lives without dulness or *taedium* that accompanies immersion in the world.[53] The steadiness of her eyes reveals her "mesure," temperance. In temperance she follows the middle way: *medium tenuere beati*. She is familiar with none, but equal to all. Her eyes do harm, but as we have seen, only to fools who desire her carnally. These persons she does not suffer gladly, but in temperance does not chide them.[54] Those foremost in pursuing her with earthly desire were always farthest from her love:

> The formest was alway behynde. (890)

Finally, she has charity, loving her neighbors, "goode folk" who are just, above all others.[55] She loves prudently, turning her affection only to those who deserve it. To sum up, the intention of the lady's heart was the intention of charity, the source of true beauty and the opposite of the amorous desire with which the Knight first approached her.

The themes already set are carried out in the description of the lady's face, indicative of the nature of her soul.[56] The Knight speaks concerning it with more truth than he knows:

> I have no wit that kan suffise
> To comprehenden hir beaute. (902-903)

The red and white of her complexion, as applied to the soul, imply her imitation of Christ, continuously re-

---

[53] See Wisdom 2.1, 8.16, 11.13.

[54] Cf. Alanus, *Summa de arte praedicatoria*, PL, 210, 161.

[55] For the meaning of these "good folk," see Alanus, *Distinctiones*, PL, 210, 913.

[56] Cf. Rabanus, *De universo*, PL, 111, 147: "Vultus autem animorum qualitatem significat."

newed in charity.[57] Among her attractions, the face is
thus especially beautiful. Its radiance, which is wisdom,[58] shines for the Knight "be hyt never so derk."
That is, the example of her wisdom is a beacon to him
in tribulation. Her face without "a wikked sygne" symbolizes an innocent soul without spot, "sad, symple, and
benygne." The beauty of the lady is thus the beauty of
charity, wisdom, and innocence, virtues which for the
Knight in his grief have become temporarily submerged.
Her speech, sweet, friendly, and founded on reason,
reveals the goodness of her soul, since in speech the
spirit is attested.[59] She was true of tongue in faith and
never used speech to harm others; she never flattered
nor chided but always adhered to the truth.

The Knight refers briefly to the other features of the
lady's body. Her neck was white and round, like the
tower of ivory in Cant. 7.4. The reference indicates that
she was an example to others, beautifying those around
her. The whiteness of ivory, symbolizing chastity or
innocence,[60] is emphasized in the lady's name:

> And goode faire White she het;
> That was my lady name ryght.
> She was bothe fair and bryght;
> She hadde not hir name wrong. (948-951)

Finally, her other physical features were harmonious

[57] Cf. Gilbert de Hoyland, *Sermones in Canticum*, PL, 184,
252: "Si sponsa es, aemulare misturam gemini coloris hujus
a sponso tuo, ut similiter candida et rubicunda sis, id est sincera
et succensa."

[58] Cf. Eccl. 8.1.

[59] Cf. Alanus, *Summa de arte praedicatoria*, PL, 210, 163:
"Qualis sermo ostenditur, talis etiam animus comprobatur."

[60] *Glossa ordinaria*, PL, 113, 1161; Bede, *PL*, 91, 1192;
Alanus, *PL*, 210, 99; *Allegoriae*, PL, 112, 882.

76

with these virtues. The description of the lady's eyes was followed by an account of the spiritual truth they reveal; the description of her face by an account of the virtue of her speech. The description of her person is now followed by an account of her actions, her "play." She was like a torch of inexhaustible brightness, furnishing a perpetual example to all others.[61] From such good example every man

> Myght cacche ynogh, yif that he wolde,
> Yif he had eyen hir to beholde. (969-970)

As the chief mirror of the feast, the lady is preeminent in good example.[62] Without her, any company would be as a crown without jewels, and without her the Black Knight is without a guide.[63] The Knight concludes by comparing his lady to the Phenix. To the Christian the resurrection of the Phenix was a symbol of hope in the Resurrection.[64] In the same way the death of Blanche should be a source of hope rather than despair to the Knight. The comparison should remind him that his lady has not died, but lives.

From the physical description of his lady, the Knight turns to an account of her virtues. In this account, the qualities which have been symbolized in the preceding description are summarized, so that the passage serves as a fitting conclusion to the description. He considers first her goodness. She was as debonair as Hester, who

[61] Cf. Matt. 13.13, and *Allegoriae*, *PL*, 112, 921, and 981; Alanus, *In cantica*, *PL*, 210, 106.

[62] *Allegoriae*, *PL*, 112, 1050: "Per speculum exempla bona. . . ."

[63] On the crown, cf. Alanus, *Distinctiones*, *PL*, 210, 830.

[64] The symbol of the Phenix became a commonplace because of the influence of the *De ave phenice* of Lactantius. See *De bestiis*, *PL*, 177, 48-49.

symbolizes mercy and humility.[65] Her intellect was directed wholly toward the good, so that she was always cheerful. In action, she was innocent, harming no one, although this innocence did not spring from ignorance. She knew the evils she avoided. Next, the Knight describes her truthfulness. In truth she was so perfect

> That Trouthe hymself, over al and al
> Had chose hys maner principal
> In hir, that was his restyng place. (1003-1005)

That is, in terms of the dreamer's vision, she had prepared her Temple well. As a "maner principal" she resembled the Virgin Mary in whose imitation she lived. She was steadfast and temperate, never deviating from the truth,

> So pure suffraunt was hir wyt. (1010)

Since she was wise in truth, her goodness followed naturally, and she did well gladly. Then, too, her will was guided by her intellect so that her heart was turned toward justice. She wronged no one, and through her righteousness prevented anyone from shaming her. She was no tyrant to her admirers, since she had no desire to enslave anyone. Nor did she deceive them with suggestions and half-truths. Finally, she made no unreasonable and unnatural demands on them,

> Ne sende men into Walakye,
> To Pruyse, and into Tartarye,
> To Alysaundre, ne into Turkye,
> And byd hym faste anoon that he
> Goo hoodles to the Drye Se

[65] See Rabanus, *In Esther*, PL, 109, 646. Cf. Machaut, *Remede de Fortune*, pp. 123-124.

And come hom by the Carrenar;
And seye Sir, be now ryght war
That I may of yow here seyn
Worshyp, or that ye come ageyn.
She ne used no such knakkes smale. (1024-1032)

She served as a good example and as a worthy object
of love, but did not take it upon herself to send men on
vain crusades. Overcome by his own recollection, the
Knight exclaims that all his love was set on her. She
was everything to him, and he was entirely hers. In
view of what he has just said, it is clear that his bond-
age is self-imposed.

The Black Knight in his youth was blind to the true
character of his lady, which his description has revealed. Because he saw Blanche only as an object of
desire she was his "worldes welfare," and his "godesse."
The dreamer, who has perceived the implications of the
description, exclaims,

Hardely, your love was wel besete;
I not how ye myghte have do bet. (1043-1044)

But the Knight insists on the uniqueness which the lady
has for him as the object of his desire.

Bet? ne no wyght so wel, quod he. (1045)

The dreamer corrects him mildly, pointing out that he
can think she is the fairest only because she seems so
to him. The implication is that the judgment is predi-
cated upon a false value derived from a self-centered
love. But the Knight's failure to understand this implication is shown in his reply: Everyone said she was
most beautiful, and his love for her was independent
of his own beauty, strength, worth, wealth, bravery,
or wisdom (1052-1074). It is significant that the vir-

79

tues the Knight lists are worldly virtues associated with pagan exemplars: he says nothing of such virtues as humility or innocence.[66] His love, he implies, was destined; he "moste nede" love Blanche (1074). This again is an excuse for sinning. He is not responsible; destiny forced him to do what he did.[67] Realizing the foolishness of this extreme excuse, the Knight hastily amends it, and in doing so admits the truth of the matter. He loves Blanche because his heart "hyt wolde" (1077). He turned to her of his own free will, for she was as good as Penelope or as Lucrece and so overcame him with her virtue. However, the Knight does not elaborate this hasty admission of responsibility. Instead he returns to further excuses. When he first saw his lady, he was young and had much to learn. Again he holds his wit responsible:

> After my yonge childly wyt,
> Withoute drede, I besette hyt
> To love hir in my beste wyse,
> To do hir worship and the servise
> That I koude thoo, by my trouthe,
> Withoute feynynge outher slouthe. (1095-1100)

The very sight of Blanche in the morning was enough to make his whole day a happy one. She has such a firm place in his heart that he would not cease to think of her for anything. In his present despair the Knight has forgotten that the virtues of Blanche, which he revealed in his description of her, were the features of

[66] Cf. the corresponding list of virtues in Machaut, *Remede de Fortune*, pp. 109 ff., where Solomon, Job, Judith, Esther, and Abraham appear along with Alexander and the rest. Chaucer has deliberately avoided Christian virtues here.

[67] See note 45 above.

her character which actually gave rise to his happiness. With his will turned to her in frustrated longing, he can only despair. Like Alcyone, he keeps the memory of his loved one as an earthly object in his heart. He cannot see that what he loved in her is immortal and that it is only as an earthly being that she is "but ded."

The dreamer interrupts for the first time with direct reference to the Knight's desperate situation:

> Now, by my trouthe, sir! quod I,
> Me thynketh ye have such a chaunce
> As shryfte wythoute repentaunce. (1112-1114)

Or, as Skeat paraphrases it, "You are like one who confesses but does not repent." As we have said, in explaining his sorrow the Knight is actually confessing. Excuses aside, he has admitted his own responsibility. If he continues to mirror in his soul only the earthly love of his lady, his confession will be worthless and false, so that no absolution may follow to bring him peace of mind. In searching his heart, the Knight must learn to place the loss of his lady in the perspective of God's Providence. He must learn to love his lady's virtues, which endure, rather than her presence, which has gone. But the Knight still understands only the suggestion that he cease to adore his lady, and he refuses to accept the suggestion:

> Repentaunce! nay, fy! quod he,
> Shulde y now repente me
> To love? nay, certes, than were I wel
> Wers than was Achitofel,
> Or Anthenor, so have I joye,
> The traytor that betraysed Troye,
> Or the false Genelloun,

81

> He that purchased the tresoun
> Of Rowland and of Olyver.
> Nay, while I am alyve her,
> I nyl foryete hir never moo. (1115-1125)

The dreamer has not suggested that he forget her, but only that he repent his misdirected love which has led him to desperate grief. The Knight's assertion that he is not like Achitophel is ironic, since Achitophel represented heresy, or turning away from God,[68] and it is precisely in turning away from the Hunter that the Knight has brought himself into despair.

The dreamer, recognizing that the Black Knight merely continues in his blindness, takes up the theme of the confession, again utilizing the terminology of circumstances. Having learned "how" and "where," he wishes to know the manner of the Knight's first address to his lady, and the circumstances under which she first knew of his love. Since the virtues of the lady as the Black Knight has described them are imperishable, he has suffered no enduring spiritual loss. To imply that the loss was merely physical, the dreamer asks again what the Knight has lost. The Knight replies somewhat impatiently, almost with the identical words that he used when the dreamer pointed out that the amount of his loss did not entitle him to immoderate grief:

> Yee! seyde he, thow nost what thow menest;
> I have lost more than thou wenest. (1137-1138)

The dreamer replies, deliberately skirting the true situation, of which he is aware. He asks whether the lady does not return the Knight's love, or whether he has

---

[68] See Rabanus, *PL*, 109, 107. Peter of Blois, p. 156, cites the followers of Absalom, such as Achitophel, as examples of false lovers, that is, fleshly lovers who abuse love.

offended her. By stating these alternatives directly he
forces the Knight ultimately to make a direct statement
of his loss. Further, the two alternatives place the
Knight's loss in perspective. Both are remediable. The
Knight can perhaps do something to be worthy of his
lady's love, or to restore himself in her grace. There
would be some point in grief over a loss which might be
remedied. But if the lady is dead, grief is pointless. The
only action possible is to turn to God.

The Knight answers the questions about the manner
and circumstances of his revelation of love to his lady.
At first she knew nothing of his love, and she remained
in ignorance of it for a long time. The Knight dared
not tell her, for fear of angering her. She controlled
him, for

> She was lady
> Of the body; she had the herte,
> And who hath that may not asterte. (1152-1155)

When a man is in such a situation he may not escape.
He wished his will to be at one with hers, so that he
did not wish to express a desire that was not hers. He
could not deny her will any more than he could his own.
On the level of the Knight's understanding, the statement is pure idolatry. Since the lady was obviously not
responsible for his capture, and since, as the Knight has
explained, she had no wish to enslave anyone, it is clear
that he was enslaved by his own desire. The complex
image involved is that of the hunt—in the false hunt
of earthly love, desire itself ensnares the heart, so that
perversely it escapes from the true Hunter from whom
by nature it should not desire to escape. When Blanche
is admired for her virtues, the love involved is charity.
This love is alone eternal and thus ultimately inescap-

able. But in his despair the Knight's love is earthly, since he longs for her physical presence. Thus he escapes from his Physician.

In recognition of his lady's example, the Knight did attempt to abandon his former mistress, idleness (797-798). But in his blindness, he succeeded only in going from one kind of idleness to another. He spent his time making idle songs. The references to Lamech and Tubal (*sc.* Jubal) are again revealing, for Lamech's three sons and one daughter, Noema, whose name is said to mean "voluptas," complete the generation of Cain which is figuratively the generation of the wicked.[69] Tubalcain wrought images in metal, and the sound of his labors at the anvil was thought to have inspired his brother Jubal, or Tubal as he was frequently called, to invent the art of music.[70] If the Knight's melodies were like Tubal's they were in all likelihood not derived from the melody which is said in *The Parliament of Fowls* (60 ff.) to come from the "speres thryes thre" but were instead harmonious with the melodies of Venus or amorous pleasure. The Knight's first song, which he quotes, has only one significant detail: the lady is "semly on to see." At this point he sees only the external beauty of the lady.

One day the Knight thought of his sorrow and of the dilemma in which he found himself:

> Allas, thoghte I, y kan no red;
> And but I telle hir, I nam but ded;
> And yif I telle hyr, to seye ryght soth,

[69] *Glossa ordinaria,* PL, 113, 101.
[70] See Paul E. Beichner. C. S. C., *The Medieval Representative of Music, Jubal or Tubalcain?* (Notre Dame, Indiana, 1954), esp. pp. 5-13.

I am adred she wol be wroth.
Allas! what shal I thanne do? (1187-1191)

This rather foolish dilemma ironically reflects that of
the Knight after he has lost his lady. The alternatives
are absurd. Unless he tells her, he is "but ded"; yet he
is afraid to tell her. In his present plight, unless he
finds her, he is "but ded"; yet he cannot find her in
any physical sense. Thus, he rightly says he knows
"no red." The solution to the dilemma in both instances
is obvious: he must speak out, facing the truth as it is.
The Knight now describes the woe he suffered because
of this "debat." Finally, he remembers that Nature is
not deceiving, so that a lady as beautiful as Blanche
must also be merciful. But he is asking for a wrongful
mercy which in fact signifies surrender to desire. For
this reason he speaks in worldly shame and distress of
spirit, making a most ludicrous figure of himself:

Bowynge to hir, I heng the hed;
I durste nat ones loke hir on,
For wit, maner, and al was goon.
I seyde "mercy!" and no more.
Hyt nas no game, hyt sat me sore. (1216-1220)

His "wit" was indeed gone. After this false beginning,
the Knight found that his "hert was come ageyn." He
has just said that "she had the herte," so that it becomes
obvious that in order to speak to her, he has to get it
back. Then with "hool herte" he beseeches and swears
and "hertely" promises

Ever to be stedfast and trewe
And love her alwey fresshly newe. (1227-1228)

His heart is now within him, yet he calls his lady his
"herte swete." The empty word-play on *heart* em-

phasizes the inherent fatuousness of his love. Although his conduct gives little promise of steadfastness, he swears it none the less. The Knight swears, moreover, that he will never be false to his lady unless he dreams, but he dreams amorously at the very moment he swears. Although he has indicated the lady's dislike of enslaving her admirers, he says to her,

> For youres is alle that ever ther ys
> For evermore, myn herte swete! (1232-1233)

She recognizes him as one hurt by her look, of whom "she ne roughte a stree" (887). The lady, whose wisdom has been attested, answers him in some detail, but he has forgotten the details because his wit was gone, and he could not comprehend them. He knew only enough to understand that "she sayde 'nay.' " At this, the Knight was thrown into sorrowful despair. "For pure fere" he "stal away," and for many a day he suffered in sorrow in his bed. In his present despair over the loss of his lady he has come full circle back to sorrow.

However, in his sorrow over his rejection by the lady, he did not abandon himself completely to despair. In another year, evidently after time for meditation on the lady's virtue and a recognition that the steadfastness of his love was more than mere desire, the Knight recovered from his callow wilfulness. There was a marked change in the heart which he wished to disclose to her. The foolish vows had disappeared, and the lady understood

> That I ne wilned thyng but god,
> And worship, and to kepe her name
> Over alle thyng, and drede hir shame,

86

And was so besy hyr to serve;
And pitee were I shulde sterve,
Syth that I wilned noon harm, ywis. (1262-1267)

The reason for this change of heart is not made explicit, but it is clear from the earlier description of the
lady. In his enforced separation from her, when the
desires of the flesh have been refused, he has learned
to love her for her virtue; he has come to a realization
of the nature of true love; he is no longer moved by
simple natural desire, but has made a rational selection
of an object worthy of love.[71] This temporary earthly
separation with its beneficent results could serve as a
model of the greater separation of her death. As the
former served to teach him the lesson of true love, so
the separation occasioned by death should bring his
heart to a realization of the ultimate love of which
true love is but a mirror, the love of God. In being
apart from her he learned to love what was true and
everlasting in her. In the separation of death, the lesson
should be made even clearer. Instead of his earlier foolishness, the Knight wished now to defend the lady's
name, to keep her from shame, and to serve her. The
relationship he desired was not physical worship but
spiritual direction. He wished her to become his spirit-

[71] Love taken simply is an appetitive force. True love, or
amicitia, involves a rational choice of a human object. See
Peter of Blois, *op.cit.*, p. 108. *Amicitia* is highly desirable, *ibid.*,
p. 116: "In rebus humanis nihil dulcius amicitia invenitur,
nihil sanctius appetitur, nihil fructuosius custoditur; habet
enim fructum vitae quae nunc est et futurae. Ipsa propria
suavitate virtutes alias condit, adversa temperat, prospera com-
ponit, tristitiaque jucundat." Finally, this love is a step toward
God, *ibid.*, p. 120: "Amicitia quidam gradus est hominibus ad
Deum. Dilectione enim mediante, homo Deo approximat, dum
ex hominis amico Dei amicus efficitur."

ual overlord. Seeing that he meant no harm, the lady granted his wish, allowing him to serve her. The ring she gave him is a token of faith to her and to the virtues she represents, an investiture which grants him the advantage of her company in return for faithful good works.[72] To his joy, the lady took him "in her governaunce," directing his youthful waywardness. He learned to share her joys and her sorrows without strife. And thus he lived guided by her virtue "ful many a yere." The example of the lady brought him from a state of childishness to a condition reflecting her own virtues.

The Knight has reached the point where the consolation open to him is clear from the context of what he himself has said. The dreamer has brought him to admit that his love for his fair White was a love for her virtues. If that is true, it follows that her death, although it is grievous, is not a cause for despair. The virtues of the lady have not died with her. The grief the poet feels in his heart is sufficiently great so that it is not easily to be assuaged, but its nature has been exposed to the intellect. He has lost nothing in comparison to that which still lives in his memory, the example of the virtue of the lady. His true love for her has been a medicine for his foolish youth. She was his physician under Christ while she was alive. In death her memory should lead him to seek the true Physician:

Pon giù il seme del piangere, ed ascolta:
sì udirai come in contraria parte
mover dovieti mia carne sepolta. (*Purg.*, 31, 46-48)

[72] The ceremony of the ring is not, of course, a marriage ceremony, which we should expect if John of Gaunt were the Black Knight. Rather, the ceremony in the poem suggests feudal investiture.

His dream began in the time of the promise of the Resurrection. The Hunter Octovyen and his hunt also afford the promise that Blanche is dead only in the body. To remind the Knight of these things, and to force him to speak plainly, the dreamer asks, "Sir, where is she now?" The Knight has already eliminated the alternative possibilities suggested in the dreamer's earlier question; the lady did not refuse him, and he did not offend her. They lived together in peace and harmony. Only one further possibility remains, but even now the Knight cannot quite make the direct statement. He says simply what he is forced to say:

> Allas, that I was bore!
> That was the los that her-before
> I tolde the that I hadde lorn.
> Bethenke how I seyde here-beforn,
> Thow wost ful lytel what thow menest;
> I have lost more than thow wenest—
> God wot, allas! ryght that was she! (1301-1307)

The meaning is unmistakable, but the dreamer persists and the Knight speaks the truth, simply, without equivocation,

> She ys ded!

The dreamer attempts no consolation,

> Is that youre los? Be God, hyt ys routhe! (1310)

The loss is a pity; that is all. The natural grief of affection is inevitable, but it is not a cause for despair. And the grief itself should vanish in time before the memory of a lady as good and virtuous as was Blanche. The important thing is to face the truth rationally in the promise of Christian comfort. In Blanche the speaker

89

had found a guide to his Physician. In his memory, even though she has died, she remains his guide. Just as her first refusal brought him to reject false love, so her death, after a temporary lapse, should bring him even closer to his Physician.[73]

In the Seys and Alcyone story, Seys says to Alcyone in her vision:

> My swete wyf,
> Awake! let be your sorwful lyf!
> For in your sorwe there lyth no red.
> For, certes, swete, I nam but ded;
> Ye shul me never on lyve yse.
> But, goode swete herte, that ye
> Bury my body, for such a tyde
> Ye mowe hyt fynde the see besyde;
> And farwel, swete, my worldes blysse!
> I praye God youre sorwe lysse.
> To lytel while oure blysse lasteth! (201-211)

Alcyone refused to recognize the implications of the statement, "I nam but ded." Immersed in her sorrow, she could not accept the idea of death, so that there was no remedy for her. When she looked up, she "saw noght." The speaker in the poem, through contemplation, has acquired intellectual instruction which enables him to see more than Alcyone saw. He has looked within himself for the image of God there, in search of his Physician. He has been reminded of the Resurrection of Christ in token of man's salvation. of the joy of the faithful in praising God, of the emptiness of false desire which leads to despair, and of the lightening of

[73] A similar attitude toward physical death appears in Boccaccio's letter "A Francesco da Brossano" on the death of Petrarch, *Opere latine minori*, pp. 222ff.

man's search by the hunt of Octovyen. Moreover, in his memory of Blanche he has seen not only her physical beauty but her virtue as well. And he has learned the nature of true love which is a step toward the Physician. In short, he has been prepared to make the admission which Alcyone refused to make.

Thus, with the simple admission that the lady has died, the search for the hart has come to an end. The rest remains simply in the healing hands of time if the bereaved turns to Christ, his Hunter:

> And with that word ryght anon
> They gan to strake forth; al was doon,
> For that tyme, the hert-huntyng. (1311-1313)

The symbolic hunt ends. Significantly, the dreamer and the Knight see the King, Octovyen, returning home to his long castle with white walls on a rich hill. The punning reference to Lancaster and to Richmond is only a small part of what is here implied:

> With that me thoghte that this kyng
> Gan homwardes for to ryde
> Unto a place, was there besyde,
> Which was from us but a lyte.
> A long castel with walles white,
> Be seynt Johan! on a ryche hil. (1314-1319)

The King is returning to his Heavenly Home, the white City of Jerusalem, on the rich hill of Sion, which Saint John described. Through the dialogue with grief, his alter ego, the dreamer, who is the poet's rational self, has turned toward his true Physician. He watches the Savior return to His home. The action which he observes symbolizes the Ascension, with its promise of the Resurrection of the just. The references to Lancaster and to Richmond, fixing at this point the historical allusion to Blanche, the Duchess of Lancaster, suggest that Blanche is among the just, and that the speaker must turn to her in memory not as an earthly figure but as a follower of Christ in the New Jerusalem. In the manner of Dante's Beatrice or Petrarch's Laura she is now at one with the Physician. As he sees the vision of Christ returning to the Heavenly City, the castle bell tolls twelve, the vesper hour which signifies the time of reward for the just in the heavenly kingdom. The sound is a promise of comfort in loss and of hope of future joy. Moreover, it brings the dream to a rounded conclusion, since the dream itself began in the "dawenynge." That is, it began at Lauds when Christ is praised for His light. There are twelve hours in the day, which is Christ, the day which begins with Lauds, the promise of the Resurrection, and ends with Vespers, the promise of the reward of the just.[74] The dream itself, which is concerned with Christ's hunt, is thus in its true structure a symbol of the Physician the poet seeks. Through it he finds the approach to the Physician he had lost at the beginning. The one physician who was his lady and the one Physician who can cure him are now united. The poet has found them both.

[74] On the morning hours of worship and their symbolism see Honorius, *Gemma animae*, *PL*, 172, 625-626: "A mane autem dicitur matutina, quasi laus Deo pro luce exhibita. . . . Hac hora Christus victor a morte resurrexit, et diem nobis ab inferis revexit, et populum sanguine suo redemptum a regno tyranni reduxit, et hostes eorum barathro immersit." For Vespers, see *ibid.*, 637: "Duodecima hora dies clauditur, et operariis jam peracto opere denarius dabitur (Matt. 20). Finis autem uniuscujusque intelligitur, cum pro transacta vita merces cuique reditur." Cf. Alanus, *PL*, 210, 812.

The Book of the Duchess

The poet wakes at the sound of the Vesper bells of his dream:

Therwyth I awook myselve. (1324)

He finds himself with the book in his hand

Of Alcione and Seys the kyng,
And of the goddes of slepyng. (1327-1328)

Since he is now in a position, through illumination, to understand the *sentence* of the story, the reference to the Seys and Alcyone story at this point is not irrelevant. Alcyone did not heed Seys' warning, "Awake!" but continued in spiritual torpor. But through his contemplative vision the speaker has awakened himself from slumber. The story provided the key to his own release from sorrow when he consulted "the goddes of slepyng" within himself. Having recovered from despair and inaction, he determined "to put this sweven in ryme." At the beginning of the poem, he was alienated from his Physician—"but that is don" (40). Now his problem has been solved: "now hit is doon" (1334).

The progression here outlined finds a clear parallel in the progress of Dante's love for Beatrice as pictured in the *Vita Nuova*. As Professor C. S. Singleton has shown, Dante first moved from earthly love to a love of Beatrice's virtues, then to a love of God through the inspiration of Beatrice. The stages are identified by Singleton with the three degrees of spiritual ascent: "This itinerary of the mind to God, as Augustine had conceived it, began, at its first level, outside of man. It turned *inward* at its second level or degree. And in its third and last stage, it rose above man. St. Bonaventura, in Dante's own century, is still tracing much the same pattern. In his *Itinerarium mentis in Deum* the stages,

93

as with Augustine, bear the names of *extra nos*, *intra nos*, and *supra nos*."[75] Like Dante, the Black Knight first looked outside of himself at Blanche's physical attractions. Being repulsed, he turned to his memory to learn the love of Blanche's virtues. Finally, like Dante, after the death of Blanche, he looks above toward the Physician whose creature Blanche is.

In *The Book of the Duchess* Chaucer celebrated the virtues of a great feudal lady with whom he was connected, either directly or indirectly. Specifically, he wrote an elegy extolling the virtues of the deceased lady, portraying the grief of the bereaved, and offering consolation. The great danger of the elegy as a type is that it becomes too complimentary for belief, or becomes trite beyond endurance, stating the timeworn obvious truths which are too general to be specifically consoling, or becomes a statement of truths which have only casual connection with the avowed elegiac purpose. In *The Book of the Duchess*, through deft use of the allegorical method with its demand that the readers or hearers heed the *sentence*, Chaucer has managed to convey a sense of personal grief over the loss of a virtuous woman and at the same time to present the great consoling truths of the Christian faith in such a way as to make them fresh and new. Above all, the poem is a graceful tribute to one of the most widely admired ladies of the English court. It is an achievement in its kind almost without parallel in English literature. However much one may be willing to admit of over-subtlety in this poem, it is difficult, once one has grasped what Chaucer is saying, to continue to patronize the book for the "something of his vivid imagination" which lies in "this relatively crude work." It is a work

[75] *An Essay on the Vita Nuova* (Cambridge, Mass., 1949), pp. 105-106.

of imagination making fresh, vigorous use of traditional symbol and truth. Its structural excellence is attested in its subtle use of repetition and in the use, for example, of the illustrative story of Seys and Alcyone as a counter-theme to the main theme of Christian consolation. The poem is thoroughly coherent. Once the symbolic context is established, the rest unfolds clearly. The problem, especially for the modern reader, is to find the one key. This found, the understanding of the poem ceases to be an exercise in ingenuity and becomes a stimulating discovery of new relationships and unexpected correspondences, of the clear and inevitable unfolding of the truths of Christian consolation.

The opening lines present the key to the poem by means of an ambiguity which, when resolved, leads to only one conclusion. The speaker is distracted to a degree that death seems a likely outcome of his grief. The portrait points on the one hand to a distracted lover, but in the figure of the one Physician who can cure the eight years' malady, the truth is shown. The speaker is one who is lost in the cares of the world. At the same time the nature of these cares is indicated by the suggestion of the lover's malady. The griefs are those of a bereaved lover who knows though darkly that his comfort cannot ultimately come from his lady. Since the circumstances of the poem were clear to Chaucer's audience, the tenor of this portrait was also clear. The speaker is suffering from his grief caused by the death of the Duchess. He is lost in worldly cares since she is gone, as was Dante after the death of Beatrice:

> Piangendo dissi: "Le presenti cosi
> col falso lor piacer volser miei passi
> tosto che il vostro viso si nascose."
> (*Purg.*, 31, 34-36)

95

He must learn that the physician who was his lady derived her curative powers from the Physician. Although the beginning of the poem seems to be chiefly concerned with the sorrow of the poet, the heart of the poem is the description of the lady. This difference between the parts of the poem, when the structure of the whole is realized, is not the result of patchwork, but of subtle craftsmanship. In the introduction a climate of belief for the eulogistic portrait is prepared through the picture of a grief which almost transcends consolation.

The desperation of the poet leads him to one of the comforts of physical sleeplessness, reading, and his reacting to a story of one whose grief refused consolation. Although her grief was for an object of infinitely less intrinsic worth than Blanche, it was to a certain extent more justified than was the poet's. Unlike Blanche, Seys did not provide a perfect example. Alcyone's despair led to the supreme folly of self-destruction over the loss of an earthly joy. Although Alcyone did not succeed in overcoming her grief, her story does suggest the proper mode of Christian conduct. The poet has an inkling of the true meaning of the tale.

The Seys and Alcyone story has significance not only as a skillful introduction to the ensuing sleep and as a foreshadowing of the theme, but also as an indication of the process by which the grieving heart may find peace. The perception of this meaning brings a kind of gaiety to the speaker, who, in spite of the heaviness of his heart, joyfully vows gifts to the "goddes of slep," for him symbolizing the faculties which give contemplative understanding. But, as in effective penance, the speaker must have the intention of effective action. His vow symbolically affords the promise that he will aspire to God. If he is granted understanding, he will effectively act to implement this understanding. The sleep and the dream ensue after a mock-serious warning that even Joseph would be nonplussed to interpret the vision.

[Skillfully contrived as to atmosphere, the dream opens with several definite symbolic indications of its purport. The room of the mind where the dreamer awakes suggests contemplation. To the ears of his mind are given the sounds of the praise of God and to its awakened eyes are shown pictures illuminated with Truth. The intellect of the speaker awakens in faith at the symbolic season of the Resurrection. He hears the horn of hope sounding the call of the hunt of Christ and His Church for the human soul. Taking his horse in preparation for spiritual battle, he encounters the hunt of Octovyen, Christ coming for the salvation of man. But the hart escapes from the effort to take the heart by strength. That is, the will of the speaker is too overwhelmed to accept at once the formal consolation of the Church. It is necessary that the hunt be pursued within the mind of the speaker, that his will be made to recognize the truth, accepting the truth for itself. The little dog, perhaps symbolic of the elucidation of the hidden cares of the human soul through example, leads the dreamer to the place of worldly concern where his will has escaped. His wilful grief is epitomized in the Black Knight, who is found leaning against the tree of despair. Through the course of a patient questioning, the dreamer brings the Knight to reveal the true nature of his grief. In doing this he reveals the spiritual grace of Blanche and demonstrates how she effectively cured him of his youthful idleness and led him into the paths of virtue.]

The poet in the person of the dreamer receives a reminder of the significant facts of the faith: the Resurrection, the Resurrection of the Just, the necessity to praise God, the necessity to look toward the light of charity, and the necessity to seek Christ the Hunter. Only in the light of faith may the true virtue of Blanche be seen and the implications of her death be appreciated.

Thus instructed, the dreamer is led to regard his own despairing will objectively. The condition of the Knight is unworthy of Blanche's memory. As a woman pre-eminent in virtue, she would have been shamed to be the cause of an unrighteous sorrow. For this reason, the grief of the Knight is treated with some humor. He is at times amusingly obstinate, but by means of a skillful interrogation he is led from a desperate attack on Fortune to the recollection of Blanche's real virtue. The portrait of the lady is itself motivated by the desire of the will to excuse itself for its temporal grief. But with this spiritual portrait as a background, we can understand his account of his own transformation under her influence from youthful cupidity to true *amicitia*. Again, with the virtues of the lady and the character of the Knight's actual love assumed, the implications of his final confession—"she is dead"—became clear. In this simple statement Chaucer achieves an extraordinary resolution of apparently conflicting elements: an appreciation of the beauty of the lady, and thus of the greatness of her loss, along with the understanding that her death was not cause for grief but for a resolution to take comfort and joy in her memory. The memory of Blanche can be revered only by turning to the Physician, the source of her virtues and exemplar of the kind of love she encouraged. The poet recovers and finds the true memory of Blanche as he sees the Redeemer returning at the vesper hour of Hope to the Heavenly Jerusalem. Blanche is dead, but in the image of Christ's Ascension rests the complementary truth that she has not died in the spirit. The dreamer awakes with the determination to set forth his vision, no longer so distraught as to be incapable of poetic activity. Even the conclusion, for all its apparent haste, contains an externally gracious compliment. The writing of the poem hinges on the poet's discovery that Blanche the Duchess remains even in death a source of inspiration.

Structurally, the dream operates on three symbolic time sequences. With reference to the Black Knight it covers the period from his early youth to maturity, a development from waywardness to responsibility. The shadow of his loss of Blanche has reduced the poet to the first of these states, but in the course of the poem he regains the latter. With reference to the ecclesiastical year, the dream develops from the period immediately following Easter to the Ascension. That is, it begins with a theme of promise, *mors Christi qua vivimus*, and ends with fulfillment. In terms of the liturgical day, there is a parallel sequence from the first hour of the day to the last, from Lauds to Vespers, from praise to final reward. Within this triple framework the dream develops through the reactions of the Black Knight as seen by the dreamer. At the outset, the Knight's situation is almost an echo of the poet's situation at the beginning of the poem, except that we are enabled through the dream to evaluate his condition in the light of Christian truth. The portrait of the lady, the central portion of the poem, serves not only its obvious function of praise, but reveals the relationship between the lady and the Physician. The beauty of the "goode faire White" springs from the same light which the dreamer saw through his windows in the dawn. Her whiteness sets off in contrast the blackness of the Knight's sorrow.

The process of the love affair reinforces the parallel between Blanche and the Hunter. Through her radiance she attracts men to the truth, hunts them for God. When the Black Knight, in misdirected desire for her physical beauty, "ruses" in desire, he is lost in the temporary despair which follows his repulse. When he looks for Blanche in his own heart and comes to see her in her true light, he finds his heart and wins the lady.

Finally, the Knight's realization of the actual nature of his love makes any added moralizing after his last confession unnecessary. In general, the technique of the poem is one in which certain truths are revealed first, and then events are described in the light of these truths. The implications, after due warning, are left to the reader or listener. Since the poem develops on the level of these implications, the ending is abrupt only on the surface. The implications which arise from what has been said in the body of the poem are more powerful than any direct statement of them could be. *The Book of the Duchess*, like all significant poetry, exists only partly in what it says. Its reality is a series of controlled developments touched off in the mind of the reader.

I I I

The Parliament of Fowls

LIKE MOST MEDIEVAL POEMS, both *The Book of the Duchess* and *The Parliament of Fowls* begin with a statement of theme. The beginning of *The Parliament of Fowls*, however, has none of the purposeful ambiguity of *The Book of the Duchess*; its initial statement is clear. The poem opens with a mocking and humorous account of the "wonderful werkynge" of Love:

> The lyf so short, the craft so long to lerne,
> Th'assay so hard, so sharp the conquerynge,
> The dredful joye, alwey that slit so yerne:
> Al this mene I by Love, that my felynge
> Astonyeth with his wonderful werkynge
> So sore iwis, that whan I on hym thynke,
> Nat wot I wel wher that I flete or synke. (1-7)

Although the poet disclaims knowledge of this Love "in dede," he has frequently read "Of his myrakles and his crewel yre" (11). He "wol be lord and syre," and "quiteth folk" unkindly, so that this lord of earthly love rivals God in wishing to have dominion over mankind. As one may read in the Old Testament of a God who performs miracles and is a God of Vengeance, so the poet has read in books of the god of Love and of his miracles and of his wrath. The poet humorously pretends to be afraid to take the name of this god in vain. He can say only, "God save swich a lord!" This is a god who, as Andreas Capellanus had put it, carries unequal weights when he "quiteth folk her hyre." The subject of the poem, then, is Love, an "unkind" lord who seeks tyrannical rule over mankind.[1] The tone is ironic.

Chaucer says he learns of Love in "bokes" which he reads often for pleasure or for doctrine. Not long before, he was reading an old book "a certeyn thing to lerne." The certain thing, as he reveals a few lines further down, is the comprehension of his true self and its happiness. When he was about to go to sleep, he was

> Fulfyld of thought and busy hevynesse,
> For bothe I hadde thyng which that I nolde,
> And ek I nadde that thyng that I wolde.

[1] The attitude taken toward inordinate love is conventional, although not always expressed with Chaucer's humor. For example, Peter of Blois, p. 132, contrasts earthly love and true love as follows: "Haec autem spuria et degenerans amicitia, quam scilicet libido contaminat, vel alterius pestis reatus incestat, delectabilius quidem ad tempus, sed perpetuo exitiales experitur affectus. Cito enim praeterit quod delectat et permanet sine fine quod cruciat. Honesta ergo et casta contrahatur amicitia; in hac enim omnia secura sunt, dulcia, pacifica, suavia, et jucunda." On the sacrilegious presumption of illicit lovers, see p. 156. "Erubescant itaque verae nomen amicitiae profiteri, qui eam vitiorum assensu vel cooperatione contaminant, et honestatis vocabulo abutentes mutuae gloriam amicitiae sibi sacrilegio praesumptione usurpant." Cf. numbers 90 and 91 in Carleton Brown, *English Lyrics of the Thirteenth Century*. See also the citation from Gavin Douglas, in J. A. W. Bennett's *The Parlement of Foules* (Oxford, 1957), pp. 191-192:
"Than is thy luiff inordinat, say I,
Quhen any creatur mair than God thow luffis."
Such love is "contrar to Kind."

The lines echo Boethius, *De consolatione*, III, Pr. 3. We quote in their context the relevant lines, which are italicized.

"Certes also ye men, that ben erthliche beestes, dremen alwey your begynnynge, although it be with a thynne ymaginacioun; and by a maner thought, al be it nat clerly ne parfitly, ye loken from afer to thilke verray fyn of blisfulnesse. And therfore naturel entencioun ledeth yow to thilke verray good, but many maner errours mystorneth yow therfro. Considere now yif that by thilke thynges by whiche a man weneth to geten hym blisfulnesse, yif that he mai comen to thilke ende that he weneth to come by nature. . . . But yif it so be that thilke thynges mowen nat performen that they byheten, and that there be defaute of manye goodis, scheweth it nat thanne clerly that false beute of blysfulnesse is knowen and ataynt in thilke thynges. . . .

"Certes, quod I, it ne remembreth me nat that evere I was so fre of my thought that I ne was alwey in angwyse of somwhat.

"And was nat that, quod sche, for that *the lakkide somwhat that thow woldest nat han lakkid, or elles thou haddest that thow noldest nat han had?*

"Ryght so is it, quod I."

Philosophy is distinguishing the gifts of Fortune from the true good which all men naturally desire. In possessing earthly goods, man is left in the state described by Boethius, having what he does not want and longing for what he has not, a certain true good. By implication, lovers ruled by Cupid seek false satisfaction so that they are "alwey in angwyse of somwhat." True joy on earth arises from the search for and the attainment of wisdom; as Hugh of St. Victor says, "The greatest solace in life is the study of wisdom; he

103

who finds it is happy, and he who has it is blessed."
The philosopher is the lover of wisdom, by which the
soul is illuminated.[2] Philosophy is the only true love.
Wisdom should be the "certayne thyng" for which
Chaucer seeks in his books.

To account for his reading, Chaucer explains:

> For out of olde feldes, as men seyth,
> Cometh al this newe corn from yer to yere,
> And out of olde bokes, in good feyth,
> Cometh al this newe science that men lere. (22-25)

Out of books comes knowledge, which the philosophers
as lovers of wisdom seek there, just as the grain of faith
comes from the field of Scripture.[3] He was reading for
"lore," seeking a useful and presently applicable *sentence.* But the book was pleasant also:

> To rede forth hit gan me so delite,
> That al that day me thoughte but a lyte. (27-28)

His book not only provided good *sentence,* but also
solas. Conventionally the pleasure which arises from a
good book, aside from that associated with rhetorical
ornament, comes from meditation over the truths it reveals, especially if they allow one to anticipate the
pleasures of the afterlife. To cite Hugh of St. Victor
again, reading and meditation are two consecutive op-

[2] *Didascalicon,* I.I., pp. 6-7. Cf. *Miscellanea,* in the works of
Hugh of St. Victor, *PL,* 177, 507: "Desiderium cognoscendae
veritatis in tantum naturale animae est, ut, quantumlibet sit
perversa, illo omnino carere non possit. Quotidianae quaestiones
indicant quod scire verum omnes cupimus. Tota vita hominis
in quaestione est. Quandiu vivimus, quaeritur."

[3] See Alanus, *Distinctiones,* *PL,* 210, 805, 695, *s.v. granum,
ager.* The image is a reflection of the basic image of the shell
and the kernel.

erations of the intellect. From actual reading we learn
the "certain thing," rule and precept; in meditation
comes the joy of consummated understanding.[4] To read
for "lore" and "lust" is to educate the soul with doctrine and to please it with meditation. Chaucer declares
that he himself, though without having attained wisdom, is a seeker of wisdom. Although the subject of *The
Parliament* is love, the poem is dedicated to philosophy,
which seeks to free the mind from earthly entanglements, such as passion.

The book he was reading was "Tullyus of the Drem
of Scipioun," which concerned human souls and their
destiny. This subject certainly belonged to the province
of wisdom, the understanding of God's laws as they affect man. Chaucer's "delite" in this book was dependent
on the joy of meditation, not on that of sensual appeal.
He promises to give his readers the heart of the book,
its *sentence*. He briefly introduces Scipio's vision and
then describes in summary the events in the book most
pertinent to its subject, the destiny of man. Scipio falls
asleep, and his ancestor African comes to him in a vision, that is, an instructive contemplative vision of the
kind afforded the dreamer in *The Book of the Duchess*.
The substance of the vision is given at once:

> Thanne telleth it that, from a sterry place,
> How Affrycan hath hym Cartage shewed,
> And warnede hym beforn of al his grace,
> And seyde hym what man, lered other lewed,
> That lovede commune profyt, wel ithewed,
> He shulde into a blysful place wende,
> There as joye is that last withouten ende. (43-49)

[4] *Didascalicon*, pp. 57-60.

Those who love "commune profyt" and are "wel ithewed" will enjoy eternal bliss. [Love of common profit is the love of one's neighbor, charity, and the opposite of self-love, the source of sin. Good customs, which are those performed in charity, will be rewarded in heaven.] The mention of the "blysful place" leads Scipio to inquiry about the immortality of the soul. He is assured that life on earth is but a "maner deth," after which "rightful folk" go "to hevene." The earth itself is small and insignificant "at regard of the hevenes quantite." Around the earth the "speres thryes thre" move in celestial harmony. In effect, this harmony reveals the Creator.[5] In the light of this vision of God's mystery, Scipio is commanded not to delight in the world, which is full of "torment and harde grace," a place, that is, where a man under the sway of the God of Love will feel his "crewel yre" and his "sore strokes." There will be a Final Day when all the deeds of men on earth will fade into oblivion:

> Thanne tolde he hym, in certeyn yeres space
> That every sterre shulde come into his place
> Ther it was first, and al shulde out of mynde
> That in this world is don of al mankynde. (67-70)

[African now gives the *sentence* of the vision, consisting of two parts, the first a positive command, the second a warning, somewhat lightly made in view of the ironically humorous purpose of the poem. Those

[5] Gregory, *Moralia, PL*, 76, 533-534. See also Rabanus, *De universo, PL*, 111, 495: "Itaque sine musica nulla disciplina potest esse perfecta: nihil enim sine illa. Nam et ipse mundus quadam harmonia sonorum fertur esse compositus: et coelum ipsum sub harmoniae modulatione revolvitur?" With "thryes thre" compare Dante's use of thrice three in the *Vita nuova*, as well as in the *Divine Comedy*.

who know themselves immortal and act accordingly
will enjoy eternal bliss:

> Know thyself first immortal,
> And loke ay besyly thow werche and wysse
> To commune profit, and thow shalt not mysse
> To comen swiftly to that place deere
> That ful of blysse is and of soules cleere. (73-77)

Man must seek after Truth. He will not find it in the
heavens themselves, but in what they reveal. He must
also look within himself to discover God, in whose
image he is made. As Hugh of St. Victor says, man
first questions the universe, to receive only the answer,
"ipse fecit nos." He must know himself "first immortal," look within himself to find the source of his
own immortality.[6] But "likerous folk," the followers
of the god of Love, will suffer in the afterworld a
punishment symbolically suited to their sin. As in life
they were blown by the gust of passion,

> brekers of the law, soth to seyne,
> And likerous folk, after that they ben dede,
> Shul whirle aboute th'erthe alwey in peyne,
> Tyl many a world be passed, out of drede,
> And than, foryeven al hir wikked dede,
> Than shul thy come into this blysful place,
> To which to comen God the sende his grace. (78-84)

The punishment is like that which afflicts the carnal
lovers in Dante's *Inferno*. Since Chaucer's poem is light
in tone, he speaks only of the lecherous who have re-
pented in time so that after "many a world be passed"
in Purgatory, "than shul they come into this blysful

[6] *De anima, PL*, 177, 171ff. Cf. the *Meditationes* printed in
PL, 184, 485ff., and Boethius, *De consolatione*, II, Pr. 5.

107

place." The theme of the *Parliament of Fowls*, as suggested in the proem, is thus the futility of earthly love. To develop this *sentence* earthly love is set off against the true love of the seeker after wisdom. The two principles stated by African establish a contrast between self-love, which leads to torment, and love of "comune profit," which leads to heaven.[7]

When Chaucer finished his book, the day "gan faylen." The night gives rest to the beasts who perform their "besynesse" without memory or reason, not judging their acts or looking to the future. But the night does not bring immediate cessation of the poet's "besynesse." He prepares for bed, "fulfyld of thought and busy hevynesse," in meditation still considering his own heart, and pondering the future. The reason for his wakefulness is that he longs for the certain thing which he has not—wisdom—and is dissatisfied with what wisdom he has. The earthly lover is like the beast in that he abandons reason, but he finds no rest in the "dredful joye, alwey that slit so yerne." The lover of wisdom is unlike the beast in that he fulfills his true purpose in the search for truth. His dissatisfaction with the world may be crowned with eternal rest.[8] The earthly lover,

[7] The purpose of the *Parliament* has an interesting parallel in the *Libro de buen amor* of Juan Ruiz, which was written to show the dangers and follies of the mad love of the world and to proclaim the true love of charity. See the introductory sermon on the theme *Intellectum tibi dabo.* . . . Cf. F. Lecoy, *Recherches sur le libro de buen amor* (Paris, 1938), pp. 22-23 and T. R. Hart, *La alegoria en el Libro de buen Amor* (Madrid, 1959). In spite of the apparent solemnity of this purpose, the *Libro de buen amor* and the *Parliament* are both distinctly humorous.

[8] For the distinction between what is appropriate to the beast and what is appropriate to man, see the *Didascalicon*, *PL*, 176,

a portrait of whom we saw in *The Book of the Duchess*, is characteristically sleepless, but the poet, weary of his day's labor, finds rest. In reward for his deep meditation, he is granted an informing vision. Since he has thought deeply of Scipio's vision, and since one tends to dream of what occupies first position in his mind, African himself appears to him to elaborate the meaning of his revelation, saying,

> Thow hast the so wel born
> In lokynge of myn olde bok totorn,
> Of which Macrobye roughte nat a lyte,
> That sumdel of thy labour wolde I quyte. (109-112)

When the solemn African has given his promise to requite the poet for his labor of meditation, Chaucer with ironic inappropriateness invokes the aid of the blissful lady Cytherea, whose torch strikes indiscriminately. She is responsible for his dream. The irony is two-fold. As the overt subject of the Valentine poem, she is the cause of his dream; she is responsible for the follies which he is ridiculing. He invokes her help as one who can best aid him, as truly as he saw her "north-north-west" when he began to write his poem. That is, she may help him not at all.[9]

African takes the poet in his dream to a park walled with green stone, to which there is a gate bearing two inscriptions. The allegorical meaning of the park must

---

743-744. See also J. A. W. Bennett, *op.cit.*, pp. 42-43, who observes that the lines echo Canto II of the *Inferno*, where Dante begins his way to Truth.

[9] See B. Bronson, *University of California Publications in English*, 3 (1935), pp. 193ff., and G. Stillwell, *JEGP*, 49 (1950), pp. 481ff. Bennett, *op.cit.*, pp. 59-60, does not consider the phrase ironic, but finds it perplexing.

be examined in the light of what has happened in the introduction, a fact which is made clear by Chaucer's explanation of the cause of his dream, that is, his reading of Macrobius. In Chaucer's account of the *Somnium*, African showed Scipio the world viewed in the light of a *sentence* containing a positive and a negative meaning. The park with the green walls should also in some way represent the world, and the messages inscribed on the gates should reflect African's *sentence*. The most basic symbolic garden is Paradise, which allegorically represents the church.[10] Specifically, the walled garden suggests the *hortus conclusus* of Canticles 4.12, taken as an analogue of Paradise, where the wall is a symbol of faith.[11] Viewed in the light of

[10] Rabanus, *De universo*, PL, 111, 334: "Paradisus, id est hortus deliciarum, mystice aut Ecclesiam praesentem significat, aut terram viventium, ubi illi qui merentur per fidem rectam et bona opera victuri sunt in perpetuum. . . . Paradisus Ecclesia est: sic de illa legitur in Canticis canticorum: *Hortus conclusus soror mea sponsa*." The Church as represented by actual church buildings frequently exhibited a message parallel to that of the last two lines of the *Quicumque vult* on either side of its main portal in the form of judgment scenes. The West Portal of St. Lazarus at Autun actually bears inscriptions. See Denis Grivot and George Zarnecki, *Gislebertus* (New York, 1961), p. 26. Wall paintings of judgment scenes on chancel arches would have had the same effect. The gate with its double inscription promising an alternative of reward or punishment as it is described by Chaucer would thus have been familiar to his audience, in spite of its poetic disguise.

[11] Concerning the wall, cf. Gilbert Foliot, *In cantica*, PL, 202, 1246: "Qua claustra? Claustro quidem fidei." For green stone, see *Allegoriae*, PL, 112, 965; or Alanus, *Distinctiones*, PL, 210, 947. It is relevant in considering the wall to recall the fact that warnings like that stated at the close of the *Quicumque vult* apply only to the faithful. Considering the nature of his audience, Chaucer would have had small need to concern himself with pagans.

final punishment or reward, Chaucer's world, as opposed to Cicero's, was the world of the church, which is in a very real sense a "garden of love." Unlike the message on the entrance to Dante's *Inferno* with its single but dire warnings, the message on the garden gate is twofold and would suggest the close of the Athanasian Creed:

Et qui bona egerunt, ibunt in vitam eternam;
Qui vero mala, in ignem eternum.

This, briefly, was the substance of African's message to Scipio. Chaucer gives the "pleyn" or full *sentence* of the inscription:

Thorgh me men gon into that blysful place
Of hertes hele and dedly woundes cure;
Thorgh me men gon unto the welle of grace,
There grene and lusty May shal evere endure.
This is the wey to al good aventure.
Be glad, thow redere, and thy sorwe ofcaste;
Al open am I—passe in, and spede the faste!

Thorgh me men gon, than spak that other side,
Unto the mortal strokes of the spere
Of which Disdayn and Daunger is the gyde,
Ther nevere tre shal fruyt ne leves bere.
This strem yow ledeth to the sorweful were
There as the fish in prysoun is al dreye;
Th'eschewing is only the remedye! (127-140)

To the truly faithful, the church is a place where the "dedly woundes" of sin are cured. As Honorius puts it, "The garden is the Church in which are the many virtues of the saints, various kinds of herbs, medicines for the various wounds of sinners." Within the church is the "welle of grace," the *fons signatus* of the Canticles, signifying God's grace in various aspects.[12] Next to this water, the tree does not wither, *folium ejus non decidet*, for there "grene and lusty May shal evere endure."[13] Who enters the gate of the church with good will finds ultimately "al good aventure." But conversely, those who enter as "likerous folk" encounter the "mortal strokes of the spere" guided by Disdayn and Daunger, which are, as we learn from the *Roman de la rose*, the enemies of foolish love. The trees do not bear fruit, and are thus unlike the tree of Ps. 1, which *fructum dabit in tempore suo*, since they do not produce the good works of charity, and the leaves of God's word do not adorn them.[14] "This strem," in contrast to the "welle of grace," leads to the "were" of the world's prison, in which the fish are "drye," that is, without the grace of the Holy Spirit.[15] The only remedy against the wrong love which leads to these misfortunes is, as Alanus said, "th'eschewing."[16] Doing well, to para-

[12] *In Cantica, PL*, 172, 423-424. As meanings of the *fons*, Honorius mentions baptism, the Scriptures, Christ, and the Church itself. In commenting on Psalm 1, St. Augustine, *PL*, 36, 68, elaborates this conception as follows: "*Fluvius Dei repletus est aqua* (Ps. 44.10). Aut secundum Spiritum sanctum, secundum quem dicitur: *Ipse vos baptisabit in Spiritu sancto* (Matt. 3. 11); et illud: *Si scires donum Dei, et quis est qui a te aquam petit; petisses ab eo, et daret tibi aquam vivam, unde qui biberit non sitiet in aeternum.* . . . (Matt. 4.10, etc.)"

[13] Cf. the garden of the Church, *RR*, 20588-20590, where the climate is always temperate.

[14] Cf. St. Augustine, *loc.cit.*, note 12, above.

[15] The fountain of cupidity is described, *Allegoriae, PL*, 112, 930. For the avaricious as captive fish, see Eccl. 9.12. On dryness, see Gregory, *Moralia, PL*, 75, 960 and 1046-1047.

[16] *De planctu, PL*, 210, 456; cf. *Anticlaud.*, cols. 570-571, *RR*, 16577-16616.

phrase the Creed, leads to life, doing evil to death. African's advice to the fearful poet, echoing Vergil's advice to Dante, indicates that since the poet is a lover of wisdom, and not a servant of the god of Love, the warning of the mortal strokes

> nys nothyng ment bi the,
> Ne by non, but he Loves servaunt be. (158-159)

He has lost his desire for earthly "lust" in his longing for wisdom, so that he can be told:

> Yit that thow canst not do, yit mayst thow se. (163)

He may gain "mater of to wryte" in looking at folly. All men are lovers in one way or another, and we may expect the garden to be a garden of love in both senses. That is, the church, or the world of Chaucer's audience rather than the pagan world of Scipio's dream, contains both wise and foolish folk.

With African leading him by the hand, the poet sees the garden within the gates. What he sees reinforces its resemblance to Paradise. He first sees trees, "with leves that ay shal laste." They are like the trees of Canticles 4.13-14, and, in being described for their uses, they suggest the bounty of Creation. The symbols of the river, the garden, and the meadow, separately and together, suggest Paradise, as it symbolizes the church. The river indicates that the church springs from the "welle of grace" and thence flows to irrigate the world. The meadow shows the church to be illuminated by the light of God's justice and adorned with the flowers of the virtues, the garden of true delight, "hortus deliciarum."[17] Like Paradise the garden contains well streams,

[17] For the river, see *Allegoriae*, PL, 112, 945. The meadow is described by Rabanus, *De universo*, PL, 111, 520: "Pratum

and because these are waters of grace the small, shining fish are not dry.[18] The birds sing and bring forth their young, following harmoniously their function of praising God and perpetuating their kind. They obey the commands of Nature, the "vicaire of the almyghty Lord," as do the many "bestes smale of gentil kynde." The garden is filled with the sound of stringed instruments, harmonizing with the sound of the wind flowing through the leaves and with the song of the birds. The harmony, like the music of the spheres, is that of God's Creation.[19] The air is temperate. All sorts of aromatic herbs grow, so that "no man may there waxe sek ne old"; it is indeed a place of "dedly woundes cure" where death does not enter.[20] It is eternal day in the garden. In short, the garden mirrors Paradise in its fullness of heavenly light and harmony.

But this garden is symbolic of the church as it should be, or as it was before the fall of man, and as it was

---

mystice intellegi potest sancta Ecclesia, vel Scriptura sacra, in quibus flores diversarum virtutum reperiuntur, et pastus spiritalis piis animalibus, hoc est fidelibus hominibus praeparatur." The description might be broken down into specific indications of the church, grace, etc., but we consider it more likely that Chaucer used a group of related symbols pointing in the same direction. The flowers and animals in Rabanus' description appear below.

[18] Cf. the "welle of grace" above. For the fish, see *Allegoriae*, *PL*, 112, 1030.

[19] On birds and their harmony, cf. above, pp. 45-46. They increase and multiply, not after the dictates of lust, but reasonably. See Gen. 1.28, and Rupert's comment, *PL*, 167, 253-255. God's command to increase and multiply is taken to mean that Adam and Eve were to multiply the faithful. On the wind, see Cant. 4.16, and Honorius, *PL*, 172, 428-429.

[20] Cf. Cant. 4.14, and Honorius, *op.cit.*, 425-426.

planned by God under the law of Nature. It is the "domus Naturae" of the *Anticlaudianus*. However, something has happened to the "domus Naturae," so that when the poet looks further, he sees details which are as out of place in Paradise as they are appropriate to the post-lapsarian world. His vision, like Scipio's, is of the world, which is a place of trial, not of physical joy, except to the mistaken who look upon it as Eve did when her eyes "were opened." Its beauty should be symbolic of its Creator, but what man makes of this beauty is his own affair.

Thus, as the poet enters upon the garden he does not come upon the Tree of Life growing beside the Well of Grace, or upon a figure like Piers Plowman guarding the Tree of Charity. Instead he sees "Cupide, oure lord," and "Wille, his doughter." They are sitting "under a tre, besyde a welle" forging and sharpening their arrows and tempering them in the well. The arrows are designed to slay or to wound. Traditionally, Cupid is the symbol of irrational love, a meaning established in the *Etymologiae* of Isidore of Seville, who calls him "daemon fornicationis."[21] The Will, who is the daughter of Cupid, must represent the misdirected will of the irrational love, inflamed by passion. Will first tempered the arrows in the well

and with hire file
She touchede hem, after they shulde serve
Some for to sle, and some to wounde and kerve.

(215-217)

[21] VIII, 11, 80. In Gothic art, the god is conventionally pictured as a young man rather than as a boy. His significance in the traditions of medieval mythography is usually harmonious with Isidore's description, and there are absolutely no grounds for thinking of him as a romantic figure.

115

Cupid's part is apparently limited to the forging of the arrows. The allegory is exact and pertinent since the arrows of desire assail man from outside, but his will gives them the temper and edge to wound or to kill his soul.[22] The poet also sees a rout of allegorical figures representing human characteristics and actions, the only figures of this kind in the poem. The figures are the artificial creations of man in society: Plesaunce, Aray, Lust, Curteseye, and so on. As artificial creations they are to be distinguished from the natural symbols of the garden.

Chaucer's garden contains descriptive materials from sources of various kinds. Some of the materials reflect Boccaccio's Temple of Venus in the *Teseida*, where, as Boccaccio's own notes indicate, the Temple is a monument to lechery. There are also materials from Alanus' description of the "domus Naturae" in the *Anticlaudianus*, possibly some from Dante's description of earthly paradise, and echoes of Biblical symbolism. The resultant garden is neither a paradise of spiritual delights nor a paradise of earthly delights, but a place like the world itself where both kinds are available. Such a garden is well designed to show that the pleasures of earthly love are deceiving and that they are a corruption of true love which is at the center of God's purpose. In the *Anticlaudianus* Alanus has as his avowed intention to show how the garden of Nature has been corrupted by man and his works. Because the paradisal garden has been corrupted by man, the poet finds himself in the en-

---

[22] Chaucer, we assume, has deliberately substituted Will for Boccaccio's Volutta since Will is clearly appropriate, and Chaucer might well have used it independently. If it is simply an error in translation, "Will" still remains an appropriate figure. See Bennett, *op.cit.*, pp. 84-86.

virons of the Temple of Venus as pictured by Boccaccio, not in the "domus Naturae" which we were led to expect.

These artificial creations have been added to Nature's domain by man through the influence of Cupid. The first figures represent the special attitudes of the earthly lover of high estate. Plesaunce represents the physical pleasures which are sought by the lover, the "plesaunce of love" associated with Venus in the "Prohemium" to the third book of Troilus. Aray is one of the conventionally prominent features of the vice of pride and a common adjunct of lechery;[23] he has the "lust present," the fleeting joy of the world in externals. He has the external Curteysie which makes his company seem desirable, the hypocritical graces of the shallow courtier: flattery, insinuation, and so on. Along with these virtues is

> the Craft that can and hath the myght
> To don by force a wyght to don folye—
> Disfigurat was she. (220-222)

This is the skill of Pandarus, of the Duenna in the *Romance of the Rose*, or of Trota Conventos in the *Libro de buen amor*, the skill of enticement or allurement which may lead another into lechery without his actually desiring it. The Delyt (Boccaccio's Van Diletto) that accompanies Gentilesse, the pleasure of the nobleman who devotes himself to earthly love, stands, like the Black Knight in *The Book of the Duchess*, alone under the oak of despair. This is the joy which

[23] Cf. Peter Quivil, *Summula*, Wilkins, *Concilia*, II, pp. 163-164; Robert de Sorbon, *De confessione*, *MBP*, xxv, pp. 352-353; *Parson's Tale*, lines 411 ff. In Gothic art, pride is sometimes represented as a young man dressed up. See Robertson, *Preface*, fig. 68.

the lover hopes to attain, but which always "slit so yerne," leaving only discontent and desolation.

[After the social graces are grouped the allurements which stimulate desire. First comes Beute "withouten any atyr," the allurement of the flesh. Then we see Youthe, symbolic of the uncontrolled and libidinous will.]These are gifts of Fortune in which the false lover is inclined to place his trust. Foolhardynesse leads to the destruction of modesty and reason, enabling the lover to forget the peril to his soul. The unscrupulous lover uses Messagerye,[24] and Meede to further his lechery. Chaucer says he refrains from mentioning "other thre," probably on the principle that "privites" should not be made known.[25] The poet sees a temple with pillars of jasper, green like the stones which make up the wall of faith surrounding the church. [But these pillars cannot be those of true faith, and probably represent the foolish faith of lovers who trust in earthly love.[26]] The temple, which is supported on the pillars of false faith, is made of brass, like copper, the metal of Venus.[27]

---

[24] Cf. R. Mannyng, *Handlyng Synne* (ed. Furnivall), 7637-7656.

[25] On this principle, see D. W. Robertson, Jr., "The Cultural Tradition of *Handlyng Synne*," pp. 172-173. The three items omitted are probably touching, kissing, and the deed itself. See *Parson's Tale*, lines 851ff.

[26] The double significance appears, for example, in Berchorius' *Reductorium Morale*. Book xiii, Chap. iv, 1, "Per virorem possum intelligere carnalitatem et carnalis vitae voluntatem"; on the other hand, "Talis color et est virtus honestatis." Jasper, Book xi, Chap. lxxxiv symbolizes faith, "quia vere ista facit hominem tutum inter omnia adversa. . . ."

[27] For an account of the metal of Venus and its significance, see Boccaccio's notes on the *Teseida*, ed. Roncaglia (Bari, 1941), pp. 421-422. The ideas in this commentary are for the most part commonplaces of the mythographic tradition so that it is not

Around the temple are always women dancing, some "fayre of hemself," and some "gay in kertels":

That was here offyce alwey, yer by yeere. (236)

These are the women who give themselves up to Venus, who "koude of that art the olde daunce." Whether fair by nature or by art, there are always many to surround the temple. On the temple are doves "many an hundred paire," appropriate symbols of amorous desire, which deceives the minds of lovers; thus they nest on the Temple of Venus rather than on the Temple of God.[28] Before the temple door sits Dame Pees, who holds in her hand a curtain, perhaps as in Boccaccio the curtain which veils the temple door through which one enters. This kind of peace is the opposite of the heavenly peace which comes after the strenuous battle against evil. It is the slothful peace of acquiescence in sin, "carnalis consensus," which Christ disclaimed. It is the negative disposition or torpor by which sin gains admission.[29] By her side is Pacience, that is, worldly patience which leads man to go on seeking, no matter what the difficulty, the satisfaction of his passions. Appropriately Pacience sits on a hill of sand, not on a rock, to indicate the vanity of the labor expended in striving for deceptive and illusory ends, in the manner of the lover who exhausts himself and his treasure. Just outside and just inside the door are Byheste and Art with the rout of

necessary to argue that Chaucer had read it. Cf. *Canon's Yeoman's Tale*, line 829.

[28] See Boccaccio, *De gen. deor.*, 3.22. Cf. Ps. 83.3-4; Lombard, *PL*, 191, 789-790. Cf. Alanus, *De planctu*, *PL*, 210, 463; Berchorius, *Reductorium Morale*, "de columba," vii, xvii, 9; Bode, *Scriptores*, p. 229.

[29] See Matt. 10.34, and *Allegoriae*, *PL*, 112, 1016.

their folk. These represent the skills indispensable to the earthly lover. To be proficient, he must know how to promise and beg, how to seduce skilfully.[30]

Inside the temple there is none of the peace of the church, only disquietude. On the altars burn fires of desire, and a continuous noise of sighs fills the edifice. The sighs of the worshipers are "engendered of desire"; their sorrows come from the "bittere goddesse Jelosye." In sovereign position in the temple stands, not Venus, but Priapus,

> In swich aray as whan the asse hym shente
> With cri by nighte, and with hys sceptre in honde.
>
> (255-256)

That is, he stands, as Ovid described him, "obscena nimium quoque parte paratus,"[31] with the sceptre of his power in his hand, but interrupted before satisfying his desires. Priapus, here pictured, represents the frustration of sexual desire, as it is typified by his own frustration at this point in Ovid's story. The men, busy bedecking Priapus with garlands of "freshe floures," obviously have allowed sexual desire to overcome their reason. The dominant god and goddess of the temple of love are Priapus and Jelosye, symbols of frustration. Venus herself is in "a prive corner in disport," with her porter, Richesse. They are "ful noble and hautayne of hyre port." The place is dark, and Venus lies on her

---

[30] In the *Libro de buen amor*, when the lover has failed three times in his attempted seduction, Love tells him that he must learn the arts pertaining to the mad love of the world. When he has learned these arts, he finally succeeds in seducing a young widow. The dialogues of the *De amore* of Andreas Capellanus also illustrate "Art" and "Byheste," although the lovers there are not successful.

[31] *Fasti*, 1.437.

bed, her golden hair bound by "a golden thred," "naked from the brest unto the hed," and the rest tantalizingly hidden by a "subtyl coverchef." By her side are Bacchus and Ceres, and two young lovers are kneeling before her, begging her help. The dark, privy corner, appropriate to the deed of darkness, her hiding from the day, her porter, Richesse, all suggest that this is the lascivious Venus, a prostitute goddess, not the servant of Nature, but her enemy. Bacchus and Ceres, who are by her side thanks to a famous verse from Terence, represent the gluttony which leads to lechery, or as Boccaccio has it, "la gulositá la quale sommamente seguonoi voluttuosi."[32] The picture of the two young devotees, praying for aid to such a goddess, tends toward the comment Theseus made in a different context, "Who may been a fool, but if he love?"

When the dreamer, leaving Venus, goes further into the temple, he sees "ful many a bow ibroke" in despite of "Dyane the chaste," memorials of the victories of Venus over chastity.[33] On the walls stories are painted which also celebrate the amorous triumphs of Love's followers. It is significant that Chaucer has arranged the details of Boccaccio's description so as to minimize the importance of Venus in her own temple. Venus' inner sanctum is the culmination of Boccaccio's description in the *Teseida,* but in the *Parliament* it is to one side in a dark corner. Priapus and Jelosye are more prominent, and the description concludes in a series of allusions to tragically fated lovers. The effect is to emphasize the fleeting and illusory character of carnal

[32] See Boccaccio's notes, p. 429. See also *Parson's Tale*, line 836, and Alanus, *De planctu, PL*, 210, 462-463.

[33] Diana is used in a similar way by Lydgate in *Reson and Sensuallyte.*

121

satisfaction and the suffering and frustration of passion. The wrongful Venus is, after all, a creation of lovers to embody their illusion that their pains will be rewarded with bliss. She is a corruption of the natural desire to increase and multiply one's kind. In pursuing this Venus, the lover is blinded by illusion, and achieves only Jelosye and the frustrations of Priapus. Chaucer's ironic minimizing of Venus does not signify her unimportance, but rather that the favors she grants are illusory when sought for themselves, and that her pervasive power for evil exists only because of the misdirection of man's will.

The dreamer has now seen the two forces which underlie the message of Scipio's vision. Those who work "to commune profit" are those who live in the garden of the church according to Nature. There they enjoy the bliss of eternal harmony in the light of charity. But the "brekers of the lawe" and "likerous folk" worship in sorrowful frustration at the temple of Venus. When the force of Venus conflicts with that of Nature, the result, as Alanus shows in the *De planctu*, is first the fall of man and afterwards the repetition of the fall in the individuals who make up the church, and finally the corruption of Nature's garden. The dreamer now returns to the garden of Nature, where he may see this conflict at work.

When the dreamer arrives at the "domus Naturae" "that was so sote and grene" (296), he sees a queen whose beauty surpasses that of all the other creatures as the beauty of the sun surpasses the stars. She is the goddess Nature, who sits "in a launde, upon an hil of floures" (302), as Alanus depicted her.[34] Assembled before her are birds of all kinds to receive judgment

[34] *PL*, 210, 490.

on St. Valentine's Day, when every fowl chooses his mate. It is usual to see as fortuitous the connection between St. Valentine and the mating of the birds, a chance uniting of Saint's day and folk legend. But in the *Passion of St. Valentine* we gain a better understanding of the relationship. The saint was one who followed strictly God's injunction to increase and multiply, that is, to increase the number of the faithful. St. Valentine illustrated in his life the marriage to Christ which increases the faithful. The true and uncorrupted mating of the birds, like that between Adam and Eve before the Fall, is also symbolic of the implementing of God's decree.[35] The assembly recalls the gathering of birds of all kinds in Apoc. 19.17, where the birds represent the faithful of all classes assembled by the Angel to put down carnal desires so as to be worthy of a place in the feast of the Lamb.[36] In the poem, the birds, whose harmony was heard when the dreamer first entered the garden, are assembled to obey in season Nature's law of generation. Their harmony indicates that they are at one with the forces of creation. Here there are no hot sighs because their desire is for

[35] See B. G. Koonce, "Satan the Fowler," *Mediaeval Studies*, XXI (1959), esp. pp. 183-184. For related symbolism in the visual arts, see A. Goldschmidt, *Der Albani-Psalter* (Berlin, 1895), p. 60.

[36] See St. Martin, *Expositio libri Apoc.*, PL, 209, 398. Chaucer very skilfully combined the Scriptural convention with the implications of a current pun on *cavea* ("bird-cage," "place of assembly") used by Bromyard in a criticism of parliaments. See John P. McCall and George Rudisill, Jr., "The Parliament of 1386 and Chaucer's Trojan Parliament," *JEGP*, LVIII (1959), note 15, pp. 279-280. The Scriptural assembly indicates generally what the assembly ought to do; the fact that the parliament is made up of birds suggests, in current parlance, that they are unlikely to be successful.

fulfillment of God's commandment, not an unnatural wish for self-gratification. The details of an illustration of Apocalypse 19.17 in the fourteenth century MS Mus. Brit. Roy. 19.B.xv help establish a relation between the Scriptural assembly and that in Chaucer's poem. In the MS the Angel, like Nature, stands on a hill with the birds arranged from the top of the tree to the ground around it. In Chaucer's assembly as in that of the Apocalypse an agent of God summons the birds to fulfill God's commandments.

Mating, or marriage, in accordance with God's law may have a generalized symbolic meaning. A bishop was by canon law "married" to his diocese, a priest was the "husband" of his flock, and anyone may be in a sense "married," whether he has an actual physical mate or not. St. Valentine's day provides a device by means of which the poet may generalize the time at which this marriage is celebrated or confirmed, whether the marriage is literal or not. The dreamer, finding himself among a great multitude of birds of all kinds, hears, instead of the "harmony" he heard at first, the harmony of created Nature, a huge "noyse," not a favorable omen for the proceedings about to take place. Nature is dressed in garments as described by "Aleyn, in the Pleynt of Kynde," or, that is, in the seamless garment of the created order, but the place of man in the garment is torn because of the activities of Venus, or, that is, because man has been more interested in the pursuit of pleasure than in marriage.[37] Although the list of birds in the *Parliament* is similar to that in the *De planctu*, there are variations in detail. Most important, Alanus does not divide the birds into four groups according to their habits of eating. Exactly where Chaucer got the

[37] *PL*, 210, 490.

124

idea for this division is uncertain, but in the *De animaliis* of Albertus Magnus birds are divided into four groups according to their habits of eating. First come the fowls which eat flesh, Chaucer's "foules of ravyne." Then, according to Albertus, come the fowls which eat worms; then seed fowls, divided in accordance with the kind of seeds they eat; and finally, the fowls which "vivunt et pascuntur in aqua," Chaucer's waterfowl.[38] The order is roughly that of the *Parliament*, where the waterfowl are mentioned before the seed fowl but are placed lowest in the dale. Albertus contents himself with merely literal observation, so that he affords no clue, beyond that implied in the order, of the meaning of Chaucer's division. For Chaucer, the fowls clearly represent men, and the fowls of ravine signify the noble class.

The simplest and most obvious actuality represented by the assembly of birds may be Parliament. Here the themes of the common profit and love are enmeshed. The Parliament deliberates and gives counsel on the common profit. Its members must choose the course which will help the King guide the state according to God's way; the birds gathered in assembly must choose their mates so that Nature's design will be carried out in accord with God's way, Nature being His vicar. How specific the analogy or historical satire is intended to be is not the question to be discussed here, but the general drift of the analogy between the assembly of the birds and Parliament may be shown.[39] In essence,

[38] Lib. 7.1.4.

[39] In the English parliament a fourfold grouping prevailed: lords spiritual, lords temporal, court officials, and commons. See May McKisack, *The Fourteenth Century* (Oxford, 1959), 182ff. Bennett, *op.cit.*, pp. 139-141, gives other evidence for the

instead of the harmony of Nature, we hear the jangling of an assembly devoted to self-interest, not to "comune profit." The corruption shown in the Temple of Venus also appears in the assembly.

Chaucer cites specifically Alanus' *De planctu*, and this poem is concerned with the conflict between Nature and the wrongful Venus, who has almost succeeded in overthrowing her order. The parliament is a development of the theme, not the details, of the *De planctu*. The virtues and vices of the various types of birds are the virtues and vices appropriate to the various classes of society living under Nature. Only since the fall has man acted contrary to nature and to the motivating principles of charity. The parliament shows how the corruption of Venus spreads from the noble birds to the other classes of society. The noble eagle, in fact, refuses to choose a mate. Instead he asks to be the "servant" in love of the formel eagle. He does not desire to "increase and multiply" in accord with God's command. Thus he asks for something which is contrary to nature and which nature does not understand. He represents those who suffer "the mortal strokes of the spere of which Disdayn and Daunger is the gyde" (135-136). The result is that the parliament is brought to a confused babble of discordant voices.

In his description of the "formel egle" Chaucer seems to have taken a hint from the *Anticlaudianus*, in which Nature, with the assistance of the virtues and of God,

---

analogy between the assembly and a parliament. The whole matter will be discussed in greater detail in a forthcoming study by Paul A. Olson. No scheme of correspondences between the various kinds of birds and the various classes of men in parliament is here suggested, although it is obvious that the birds of prey represent the lords temporal.

creates a perfect man to combat the vices. In the formel
eagle Nature has created a woman in whom "was everi
vertu at his reste." She is

> of shap the gentilleste
> That evere she among hire werkes fond,
> The moste benygne and the goodlieste. (373-375)

[If a male eagle were found suitable to her in virtue,
their marriage would serve as a guide and model for
good conduct. This ideal marriage is frustrated through
the self-seeking of the noble suitors and through the inability of any in the whole assembly to point out what
is wrong clearly and convincingly.]

Insofar as Nature is concerned, the choosing of a
mate involves simply the selection of an object of
sexual desire so that her function of "multiplication"
may be implemented in an orderly way. Her prelimi-
nary exhortation to the assembly involves the salient
principles of natural law as it concerns mating. In the
first place, the order of choice is based on the natural
order of society which is a basis for the positive law,
in accord with which those in more responsible positions
requiring greater wisdom are placed first. The royal
eagle, the prince, is to have first choice, and after him
the rest shall choose "by order," after their "kynde."
Whether a given choice is successful depends on "hap"
or Fortune. A wife is a gift of Fortune, not a gift of
God or Nature. Nature wishes that he who is most involved in love or who feels most strongly the motion of
the senses imparted by her wayward helper Venus will
get, not necessarily the one whom he most loves, but
the one who best loves him (403-404). This wish emphasizes the principle of consent. [For a man to love
strongly one who reluctantly returns his affections leads

127

only to frustrations which disrupt Nature's harmony.
She insists

> That she agre to his eleccioun,
> Whoso he be that shulde be hire feere. (409-410)

In other words, in the natural order of things, the
customary hierarchy of society is to be observed; mates
are to be paired after their "kynde," and the female
should always consent to the attentions of the male
who is her "feere." These rules are well designed to
preserve the harmony of creation, for they obviate
quarrels over precedence, unfruitful and unhappy mat-
ings, jealousy, and the discordant acts of seduction and
rape.

Nature is the vicar of God on earth in knitting together elements in accord. As a part of her function in
maintaining the harmony of creation, she carries out
true mating as she best can. Her injunctions impress the
need for order and suitable choice. If man still lived
under natural law alone, these injunctions of Nature
would suffice, but since the Fall, Nature's rule must be
implemented by positive law administered by man, and
made effective through grace. When the natural order
does not function smoothly, as since the Fall it seldom
does, God's grace is needed to set it right, such grace as
is manifested in this poem by St. Valentine. The parliament of birds is thus called upon to settle the dis-
pute of the eagles, that is, the frustration of Nature's
plans through the influence of the wrongful Venus. The
parliament has the obligation to suggest a rational remedy which will be in accord with Nature and with God.
The responsibility is not Nature's; it is theirs, acting
through grace.

Nature is justifiably proud both of the formel and of

the tercel eagle. Her intention that they mate is clear, but may be frustrated by a lack of desire or a misdirected desire on either part. The royal eagle in fact desires the formel; but because he is a follower of the wrongful Venus, he cannot act upon Nature's intention with a correct and natural offer. Obedient to the commands of Venus, he will have his lady "soverayn," not his "fere" as God created her. Instead of the wife and companion which Nature ordained as proper, he wants a sovereign lady. The eagle chooses "with wil, and herte, and thought" the formel eagle on Nature's hand, giving to her the devotion which he owes to God, swearing to be hers completely and to do her bidding to death. He asks of the formel "merci" and "grace" with death as an only alternative. She has the power to make him "lyve" or "sterve." Thus he places her in the supreme position which should be reserved for God. He makes the standard protestations: if she does not consent to be his, he will die; he suffers greatly; he will be forever true, obedient, and active in her service; he will never boast. If he fails in the vows, he asks to be put to death. Why should the formel love him? Apparently not content with Nature's assumption that the formel will have him because he is worth having, he declares that she should love him because he loves her more than anyone else does. That is his only claim, a claim which reverses the order of Nature's wish that the male join the female who sighs for him most. The speech in all its exaggeration is, moreover, a profession of idolatry. The first speaker, the one who should be an example to the rest, sees the formel eagle, in which all virtues are at rest, merely as an object of physical desire. In abasing himself before her, he reveals himself as one prepared, as it were, to bedeck Priapus with garlands, breathe the sighs of Jealousy, and kneel before the wrongful Venus. The outwardly attractive and highly "civilized" words merely disguises the unnaturalness of his procedure.

The formel blushes for shame and makes no reply:

Ryght as the freshe, rede rose newe
Ayeyn the somer sonne coloured is,
Ryght so for shame al wexen gan the hewe
Of this formel, whan she herde al this. (442-445)

If she were not Nature's beloved creature, as she is, her blush could be put down simply to maidenly coyness, instead of a natural "shamefastness," but, desiring a mate, as she does, she blushes because she is faced with something unnatural which bodes ill for any rational mating. She cannot say "yes" to such an offer without condemning herself to be a servant of Venus. Virtuously natural, she is forced to say "no," or to permit herself to become an earthly idol, to accept an unnatural worship. At the same time, she is unable to say "no," since it is clearly Nature's wish that she mate with the royal eagle. If the royal eagle's offer had been manly and honest, she could, with maiden blushes say "yes." But the foolishness of the eagle leaves her ashamed and confused, uncertain of her true course.

Moreover, the royal eagle's failure to claim her hand on the rational ground that he most deserved to win her opens the way to other claims which are as valid as the eagle's because they are equally grounded in a longing for a relationship which violates the hierarchy of Nature. The tercel of lower kind establishes a claim to the formel in that he has served her in his degree longer than has the royal eagle. He is ready to vow the same standard vows as has the royal eagle. The formel is placed in an even greater difficulty than before in making known her own desires. Now she cannot choose simply on the basis of worth and delight but is asked to judge between two claims, neither of which is rational. The first claims to love her more than anyone else. The second denies this claim in protesting that he has served her longer. Still a third eagle takes advantage of the opening made by the royal eagle. His argument serves to reinforce the irrationality of the first two. He has not served her at all, but still he is her "treweste man" and "faynest wolde hire ese" (479-480). There is obviously no way to tell whether one suitor loves her more than another. All three eagles base their claims not on any consideration of how the formel eagle may profit by marrying them but on the claim of personal suffering. They profess humble service but are actually concerned with satisfying their own desire, and for the degree of such desire there is no natural or rational measure.

⌈The self-centeredness of the three eagles is further revealed as their "gentil ple"⌉ continues "from the morwe . . . tyl dounward drow the sonne wonder faste" (489-490). They seem unaware of the principle of *noblesse oblige* until finally "the noyse of foules for to ben delyvered" bursts forth. The unnatural, prolonged, and irresolvable debate of the noble birds causes the beginnings of insurrection. Their selfish demands on the patience of the other members of society have been sufficiently great as to appear tyrannical. The fowls, in violation of the precedence established by custom and by Nature, cry out:

Have don, and lat us wende! . . .
How sholde a juge eyther parti leve
For ye or nay, withouten any preve? (491-497)

131

Unlike the self-deluded noble suitors, they are aware
that no proof of inner passion may be offered. The
confusion is so great that the dreamer thought "the
wode hadde al toshyvered." All remnants of paradisal
harmony are gone; the voices of the birds become a
noisy chatter:

> The goos, the cokkow, and the doke also
> So cryede, "kek kek! kokkow! quek quek!" hye,
> That thourgh myn eres the noyse wente tho.
>
> (498-500)

The goose, who like the Wife of Bath knows of reme-
dies of love the old dance and is not hesitant to flout
authority, speaks up with an unsolicited offer of advice
on behalf of the waterfowl. Moved by the example of
the goose, the cuckoo, self-appointed spokesman of the
wormfowl, offers to resolve the difficulties of the situation. He makes an assertion of his own authority, al-
leging as his motive the "comune spede" which, as we
learned in Scipio's vision, is the chief concern of the
righteous (74-75). The phrase "myn owene auctorite,"
which the cuckoo uses, has an inappropriate officious-
ness about it. In view of what Chaucer says about the
cuckoo, "ever unkynde" and "fol," we may justly regard these remarks with suspicion. They have a hypocritical air. The turtle apparently perceives the hypocrisy latent in the pretensions of the cuckoo. There is
otherwise no reason for her great anger, and she displays a natural humility in contrast with the bumptious-
ness of the goose and the arrogance of the cuckoo:

> I am a sed-foul, oon the unworthieste,
> That wot I wel, and litel of connynge.
> But bet is that a wyghtes tonge reste

132

Than entermeten hym of such doinge,
Of which he neyther rede can ne synge;
And whoso hit doth, ful foule hymself acloyeth,
For office uncommytted ofte anoyeth. (512-518)

The cuckoo should be still, since he knows nothing of the true character of a debate dealing with matters about which he can neither "rede" nor "synge." In effect, the turtle-dove challenges his authority to intervene. The turtle protests that the cuckoo took upon himself an office which had not been committed to him. [She is defending the prerogatives of the noble fowls, their right to carry on their affairs without questioning by the lower orders of birds.]

At this point, Nature intervenes sharply to halt the quarrel which she recognizes to be unnatural. She insists that the problem be solved in an orderly fashion. She will "consayl fynde" of the orders of the birds themselves represented by their spokesman. The noble birds elect the tercelet of the falcon in "pleyn eleccioun." Their spokesman is to act in the formal capacity, as they feel, of the *magister* in a debate, for it is he who will "diffyne al here sentence," that is, distinguish the true from the false in the substance of their argument. Finally, he will "termyne," or render an authoritative conclusion.[40] The tercelet of the falcon is presented to Nature, who presides over the parliament. She accepts him "with glad entente." The formality of the procedure is in keeping with the understanding by the nobility of correct governmental etiquette. The tercelet gets to the heart of the difficulty in the debate, its essential unreasonableness:

[40] See B. F. Huppé, *JEGP*, xlvii (1948), pp. 334-342; and Bennett, pp. 139-141.

The Parliament of Fowls

Ful hard were it to preve by resoun
Who loveth best this gentil formel heere;
For everych hath swich replicacioun
That non by skilles may be brought adoun.

(534-537)

But his own proposals reflect the beliefs and prejudices of his class. They are based on principles of inherited "gentilesse," and chivalry. Since it is impossible to determine "by resoun" which eagle loved the formel best, the only solution is "batayle" (539). But when the eagles announce themselves ready, he insists that they have interrupted him before he has completed his judgment. It is necessary for them to submit to the voice of the parliament. If there were a battle, it would be decided in favor of the best knight. But since the identity of the best knight is already known, there is no need for battle. It is fitting that the lady accept the royal eagle. Knighthood, estate, and blood clearly favor him. From the point of view of worldly "gentilesse," quite apart from true "gentilesse" of virtue, the royal eagle should have the formel.[41]

Although superficially in accord with Nature's plans, the argument is actually not based on the "comune profyt." Knighthood, estate, and blood set off the noble classes above the rest. The tercel, in appealing to these things, shows that he supports the artificial distinctions of his class. His position as a nobleman causes him to overlook the fact that the love avowed by the three eagles can lead only to confusion. They do not seek simple mating as prescribed by Nature, wherein

[41] See the discussion of "gentilesse" in Chaucer's poem on the subject, or in the Wife of Bath's Tale. The history of this concept and its significance in the work of Chaucer will be treated in a forthcoming study by Alan Gaylord.

sexual gratification is concordant with the law of increase of kind, wherein there is order as between the sexes. What they seek is an unnatural refinement of passion, the illusion of a self-sufficient, self-justifying love, wherein sexual gratification is perverted from its proper function, and wherein the male becomes the suppliant, rather than the guide! Such confusion cannot be remedied by appeal to still other worldly considerations like birth and honor.

With much less formality each waterfowl speaks in turn his "large golee," supporting the goose in her pretensions to be their spokesman because with her "facounde gent" she "so desyreth to pronounce" their "need." They seem to elect the goose more as if they had been won to accept her by the insistence of her claims than through any reasonable desire to have her speak. In "hire kakelynge" she first takes care to indicate her own authority and worth:

> Pes! now tak kep every man,
> And herkeneth which a resoun I shal forth brynge!
> My wit is sharp, I love no taryinge. (563-565)

Her advice after the preamble in self-glorification, consists of one line:

> But she wol love hym, lat hym love another! (567)

Let him ask the lady. If she says "no," let him ask someone else. She sees something of the foolishness of the eagles' conduct, but she is blinded by her own lusty desires so that she does not understand what causes the eagles to engage in their long foolish debate.[42] She can

---

[42] Berchorius, *Reductorium morale*, VII, viii, calls the goose "animal libidinosum," which is like lechers "quibus non potest sufficere infinitas mulierum." The duck, VII, vii, is similarly described, but, unlike the goose, only *in malo*.

see only that they want one thing and seem to be asking for another. Let them ask for the right thing. Like the goose, the eagles are drawn by passion, but unlike the goose they transform the object of their passion into an idol to worship. The goose is not concerned about what the eagles want; she is concerned only about their failure to do anything about it. The attack of the goose on the refinements of noble conduct provokes an immediate rejoinder by the sparrowhawk. Without answering her argument, he calls her "fol" to the accompanying laughter of the other noble birds.

The seedfowl without apparent debate select the turtle, who has already acquitted herself well,

> And preyeden hire to seyn the sothe sadde
> Of this matere, and axede what she radde.
>
> (578-579)

Unlike the birds of ravine, who are interested in technical competence, or the waterfowl, who are impressed by the ready and noisy tongue of the goose, the seedfowl ask for the "sothe sadde." Their election of the turtle is decorous, as is her acceptance. She would make clear her intent and meaning. It is with serious and considered purpose therefore that the turtle speaks,

> Nay, God forbede a lovere shulde chaunge!
> The turtle seyde, and wex for shame al red.
>
> (582-583)

The voice of the turtle speaking of love reminds us of Cant. 2.12, which was taken to advocate heavenly love, as St. Bernard explains, it "doceat nos terrena despicere et amare coelestia."[43] The turtle's remarks as interpreted in one way present the true solution to the prob-

[43] *Sermones in Cantica*, PL, 183, 1064-1065.

lem; man's love should be directed toward overcoming earthly entanglements and gaining heaven. The turtle answers the argument of the goose:

> Forsothe, I preyse nat the goses red,
> For, though she deyede, I wolde non other make;
> I wol ben hires, til that the deth me take. (586-588)

If the love of the royal eagle were natural and rational, if his service were the service of true virtue rather than worldly virtue, this would be excellent advice. Under the circumstances, however, it merely strengthens the royal eagle in his folly. To serve her is all he wants of his "soverayn." Her consent to such attentions would never make a marriage of the relationship. The solution to the problem rests in true marriage, encouraged by Nature and blessed by God. Whereas the argument of the goose supports mere physical satisfaction, the argument of the turtle, whether through innocence or guile, supports a kind of faith which may be virtuous in one context but idolatrous in another. The turtle's voice is heard in praise of fidelity in marriage, perhaps even in praise of the love of God, but the praise misses its mark in the parliament, for it is inappropriate to the eagle's subversion of Nature's mating by his demand that his love escape from the hum-drum of the natural, into the "romantic" realm of Venus' priapic temple of elegant frustration.

The duck reiterates the position of her sister, the goose, in answer to the turtle, speaking out of turn and again disturbing Nature's order. The duck sees in the romantic passion of the noble suitors only the absence of any sure principle for the satisfaction of desire:

> That men shulde loven alwey causeles,
> Who can a resoun fynde or wit in that? (590-591)

137

Of course, the duck is right, but for the wrong reasons.
This is a causeless love and thus an irrational one, but
in love the duck refuses to find anything but a physical
desire that does not demand an over-refined selection:

> Ye quek! yit seyde the doke, ful wel and fayre,
> There been mo sterres, God wot, than a payre!
> (594-595)

This assertion arouses the "gentil" tercelet to a vigorous
rebuke:

> Out of the donghill cam that word ful right! (597)

Since the duck does not know the nature of love, like
the owl she is blind to the light that illumines the eyes
of the idolatrous lover as he gazes on his mistress. Once
the attitude of the noble suitors has been attacked, the
other noble birds persistently defend them.

Unlike the other orders, the wormfowl are not represented by a legally elected spokesman. The cuckoo has
no need to be elected, but simply pushes his way for-
ward:

> Tho gan the kokkow putte hym forth in pres
> For foul that eteth worm. (603-604)

Here the hypocrisy of the cuckoo's first statement is revealed. The bird who lays his eggs in other birds' nests,
who cares nothing for his children, is a type of avarice
and foolish speech; he actually has no concern for common profit so long as he gets what he wants:[44]

[44] Cf. Neckam, *De naturis rerum*, p. 117: "Cuculus frequenti
ejusdem soni inutili repetitione taediosus nugator avaritiae
typum gerit, proclamantis et dicentis, 'Affer, affer.' " Berchorius,
Reductorium morale, VII, xxviii, because of the cuckoo's repeating the sound of his own name likens it to "iactatores et
vanigloriosi qui scilicet alta voce praedicant laudes suas. . . ."

So I, quod he, may have my make in pres,
I reche nat how longe that ye stryve. (605-606)

So long as his needs are supplied in the same slothful
peace which stands at the door to Venus' Temple, he
is careless of his obligations to the common profit. Of
all the birds the cuckoo most openly professes his self-
seeking. His remedy has no value and seems merely a
product of impatience:

Let ech of hem be soleyn al here lyve! (607)

The suggestion is without the saving grace either of the
goose's practical remedy or the turtle's poetic one. The
final remark to the effect that his "shorte lessoun"
needs no record, since it may easily be kept in mind, is
in keeping with the cuckoo's pomposity. At the same
time it is an inadvertent admission that his own self-
seeking is so evident that it need not be recorded. The
merlin's reply is well taken. It represents the first serious personal attack of the parliament:

Ye, have the glotoun fild inow his paunche,
Thanne are we wel! seyde the merlioun;
Thow mortherere of the heysoge on the braunche
That broughte the forth, thow rewthelees glotoun!
Lyve thow soleyn, wormes corupcioun!
For no fors is of lak of thy nature—
Go, lewed be thow whil the world may dure!
(610-616)

Nature realizes that the parliament has become discordant and futile, with the whole breaking down into
a series of personal arguments and with no one offering
advice for the common good:

139

Now pes, quod Nature, I comaunde heer!
For I have herd al youre opinyoun,
And in effect yit be we nevere the neer. (617-619)

She decrees that the formel have her choice and that her
decision be final. As the terclet has pointed out, there is
no way to determine which eagle loves the formel best,
so that the only solution left is to allow the formel to
choose. The principle of consent is restated emphati-
cally, for it is the basic principle which Nature supplies:

Thanne wol I don hire this favour, that she
Shal han right hym on whom hire herte is set,
And he hire that his herte hath on hire knet.

(626-628)

She shall have the one she desires, and he shall have the
one he desires. Nature's statement is optimistic in view
of the difficulties which have been encountered in furthering her master plan. But Nature knows no other
solution than that the fowls mate in accordance with
natural inclination. She has regard, as she said, only
for such mating. She is no respecter of rank as such,
she says, obliquely replying to the proposition of the
tercel that the mating of the eagles should be in accord
simply with dignity and worth as the noble class understands them:

Thus juge I, Nature, for I may not lye;
To non estat I have non other ye. (629-630)

Although Nature has to do only with the suitability
of desire, she is ultimately guided, as God's vicar, by
the necessity for Reason and Grace in any proper mating. Nature is, of course, not herself Reason. The character of the assembly is such as to indicate that Reason

is absent. But if Nature were Reason, she says, she
would counsel the formel to take the royal tercel:

If I were Resoun, certes, thanne wolde I
Conseyle yow the royal tercel take,
As seyde the tercelet ful skylfully,
As for the gentilleste and most worthi,
Which I have wrought so wel to my plesaunce,
That to yow hit oughte to been a suffisaunce.
(632-637)

Reasonable choice would seem on the surface to dictate
that the formel and royal eagles be mated. But Nature's
reasons for the choice are not themselves reasonable.
They ignore the positive evidence which the folly of the
eagles has demonstrated. It is clear that Nature does
not understand either the idolatry of the eagles or the
blind haste of the waterfowl. As unnatural aberrations
from her basic principle of moderation and order, they
are beyond her province. She can see that the parliament
is futile, but she cannot understand that the reason for
this futility is the self-seeking which corrupts it from
the eagles on down. Nature cannot remedy what is unnatural. That remains for God and for man guided by
His grace and working in accordance with the reason
that God has given him. All Nature can see is that both
the royal eagle and the formel are well-made creatures
of about equal rank and that their union seems natural.
She leaves the decision to the formel, but the formel
cannot choose because she has neither nature nor a rational choice to guide her.[45] Since she is always under
Nature's "yerde" and knows herself to be fully Nature's
creature while her life may endure, she can simply rec-

[45] In the *Anticlaudianus* Nature must call upon the virtues and
upon God Himself to create the virtuous man.

ognize the situation that confronts her as unnatural. As a female interested in mating, the formel can only reject what is unnatural, i.e., both Venus and Cupid. She asks, therefore, for a year's grace:

> Almyghty queen! unto this yer be gon,
> I axe respit for to avise me,
> And after that to have my choys al fre:
> This al and som that I wol speke and seye.
> I wol nat serve Venus ne Cupide,
> Forsothe as yit, by no manere weye. (647-653)

Perhaps she hopes that the tercelet will abandon romantic passion in favor of simple mating. Unaware of the full implications of the situation, and unable to remove Venus and Cupid from their control of man's desires, Nature grants the formel's request. She advises the tercelets to endure and serve for a year, each taking pains "for to do wel." Meanwhile the rest of the birds are free:

> And whan this werk al brought was to an ende,
> To every foul Nature yaf his make
> By evene acord, and on here wey they wende.
> (666-668)

The three eagles are alone left unnaturally without mates, and their folly causes the formel too to be alone left without her mate, until the eagle in the course of the year may abandon his perversity.

The rest of the birds take their mates in "blisse and joye." The lecherous waterfowl, the faithful seedfowl, and the wormfowl led by the avaricious cuckoo all find a solution to the problem of what to do about the motions of Nature's helper, Venus. To all of them the solution is simple and full of bliss and joy. After all, this is

a society of birds in which through poetic license the
perverse folly which afflicts mankind has been allowed
to appear. The mating of the birds may be analogous to
marriage, but is not to be confused with it. As fowls are
not, in fact, disturbed by romantic passion, human
beings cannot, in fact, mate in birdlike simplicity of
natural fulfillment. The birds are happy in their mating, but the question remains whether for men such joy
represents the lasting joy of the truly married or the
joy of the worldling which "slit so yerne." In his humorous Valentine's Day poem, Chaucer does not linger
with the problem. He is content simply to show that the
birds are happy in fulfilling Nature's impulses in matri-
mony and that only the worshipers of Venus remain
unsatisfied and sterile. They have created momentary
chaos in the society of birds, disrupting Nature's harmony and bringing into their society unnatural vices
beyond the understanding or cure of Nature. The
dreamer has seen the results of what would happen if
birds were afflicted by the contrary claims of Nature
and Venus. Through this vision he understands why
Nature's garment is torn in the place allotted to man.
It is the "wonderful werkyng" of love.

As the song of the birds which is heard in the earthly
paradise is a harmonious song in praise of God, the
discord and cackling which we hear in the assembly of
the birds is a sign of the corruption of that harmony.
The Valentine song which the birds sing recalls in its
method the inscription over the gate and is clearly related to man. The wording of that inscription suggests
the rewards and punishments which the earthly lover
sees in his blindness, but the actual meaning is concerned with eternal reward and punishment. Although
the Valentine song, on the level of sense with relation

143

to the life of birds, simply suggests the gladness of the
birds in early spring welcoming the warmth and light
of summer, rejoicing in the thought that cold winter
with its darkness will be over, the song is, in fact, in
praise of a human being, Saint Valentine, the martyr
who evidenced in his sainthood the power of God's
grace to lead men out of the "wintres weder" of the
world, out of the "longe nyghtes blake," of worldly
ignorance and frustration, into the "somer" of God's
Kingdom.[46] For his sake a chosen chorus of birds, "ful
blissful mowe they synge," celebrate him, and his example, and in so doing restore, for a moment, the harmony of Nature's garden. For men their song suggests
that it is by an appeal to God's grace alone that the
rent in Nature's garment may be repaired. The solution
to the problems raised by Cupid and Venus is marriage,
not idolatrous love.

Chaucer leaves no doubt of his own position. He is
awakened, not by the song but by the shouting "that
foules maden at here flyght awey." The shouting suggests rather the parliamentary turmoil of the world-
lings than the contemplative calm of the heavenly song.
The lesson of the poem is like the lesson which African
learned: the vanity of the world and of the lovers of the
world. Having seen this vanity clearly, Chaucer repeats
the avowal he made at the beginning of the poem:

Of usage—what for lust and what for lore—
On bokes rede I ofte, as I yow tolde. (15-16)

[46] See *Allegoriae, PL,* 112, s.v. *estas, hiems, nox*; see also
Rabanus, *De universo, PL,* 111, 303, etc. The imagery was
thoroughly conventional throughout the Middle Ages. Further
discussion will appear in Huppé, *A Reading of the Canterbury
Tales.*

The Parliament of Fowls

Now he says,

I wok, and othere bokes tok me to
To reede upon, and yit I rede alwey.
I hope, ywis, to rede so som day
That I shal mete som thyng for to fare
The bet, and thus to rede I nyl nat spare.

(695-699)

Reading is the symbol of the good life. It delivers the mind from the spears of desire and lifts it to the truth of heaven.[47] Chaucer hopes to follow wisdom.

[47] Cf. Alanus, *Summa de arte praedicatoria*, PL, 210, 180:
"Lectio sensum acuit, intellectum multiplicat, animositatem discendi parat, facundiam ministrat, teporem mentis calefacit, torporem expellit, tela libidinis exstinguit, gemitum cordis excitat, lacrymas elicit, Deo nos propinquos facit. Amorigraphus ait:

Otia si tollas, periere Cupidinis arcus.

Si legis, effugiat otium, diabolus te invenit occupatum."
Richard de Bury, *Philobiblon* (ed. Altamura), 15. 9-15, expresses similar ideas in terms of "philosophy": "Hic autem amor philosophia greco vocabulo nuncupatur, cuius virtutem nulla creata intelligentia comprehendit, quoniam vere creditur bonorum omnium mater esse (Sapientie VII°). Estus quippe carnalium viciorum quasi celicus ros extinguit, dum motus intensus virtutum animalium vires naturalium virtutum remittit, ocio penitus effugato, quo sublato 'periere Cupidinis arcus omnes.'" In devoting himself to reading, Chaucer is, in effect, avoiding the operations of "Cupide, oure lord," and staying well away from the Temple of Venus with its jealous sighs and Priapean frustrations. It was reading which enabled him in the first place to see these things in their proper perspective and to describe them for his readers. That is, the final statement about reading is thematically an integral part of the poem and is neither merely decorative nor merely autobiographical.

The Parliament of Fowls

[The solemnity into which our exposition has stumbled is not intended to reveal the *Parliament* as itself solemn and humorless. Rather it is an inadvertent admission of the great intellectual distance between ourselves and the audience for which the poem was written. The details of Christian faith, of which we find it necessary to remind ourselves, were part of the intellectual foreground for Chaucer and his contemporaries. Aberration from patterns clear, ordered, and omnipresent in men's lives offered the basis for medieval humor.] When the contrast between illicit love and love in accord with God's order is absolutely clear, the solemn nonsense of the protestations of the irrational lover, the absurdity of his sufferings, and the foolishness of his hot desires are equally clear, and are a perennial subject for medieval laughter, especially when there is something in every one of us which warns that the lover's foolishness may be our own. Against the medieval order the aberration stood out with a clarity not always present for us.] We might explain the presence of the sober-sided Scipio in a Valentine poem, but unless effortlessly we see in Scipio what Macrobius saw in him, a guide to the understanding of man's origin, or what Chaucer saw in him, a guide, like Vergil, to be interpreted in the light of Christian revelation, unless we see this at once in Scipio, the humor which finds Chaucer invoking the aid of Cytherea in the course of being guided by Scipio, the humor which reveals Cupid at the heart of Nature's garden, tends to escape us. Or before this, unless we are certain in our minds that all human love for the distractions of the wayside is absurd if it is taken seriously, we will miss the humor of the opening lines of the poem and of the exclamation "God save swich a lord!"

146

The Parliament of Fowls

The certainties which we have found it necessary to labor are the certainties which are basic to the humor of the poem. The frivolous combination of mockery and romantic sentiment which still characterizes the exchange of Valentines was to the medieval Christian a symbolic counterpart of St. Valentine's serious function. The lechery of the goose, the self-seeking of the cuckoo, and the folly of the eagles stand revealed only when seen against this function. More broadly, Chaucer's poem, with its mocking and humorous attack on Venus and Cupid, achieves its humor through the clarity of the medieval concept of love finding its fulfillment not in itself but in its accord with God's law of charity. The parliament of the birds remains in part amusing for us because it reflects a consistent human weakness for gabble. But if we see it in the clear light of what it has corrupted, the order of man as established by God and administered by Nature, the parliament appears not merely lightly amusing, but rises to high comedy. The Valentine song of the birds is pretty. That remains no matter what we have lost of Chaucer's medieval view. But above this prettiness may be found, through the medieval certainties, the high comedy which comes in seeing without tears the folly of man who can sing of the love of God and yet choose blindly to cherish the summer of his earthly joy. The medieval certainties having become the doubts of our modern world, we take seriously the affairs of the heart and of the self which seemed very unimportant to the medieval Christian, except as matters which betrayed and ensnared him. There is tragedy for us in Matthew Arnold's cry, "Ah, love, let us be true to one another!" For Chaucer this cry, if taken literally, would appear either amusing, or pathetic through human sympathy

147

for the lost worldling. Laughter was a device valuable then as now to restore in man a sense of proportion. For the Middle Ages, the sense of proportion consisted in seeing that human passion is trivial; in seeing that there were no fools so great as the worldly wise, the sophisticated who had learned the notes of the Siren's song until their own ears were charmed. Meanwhile men continue to pile worldly miseries upon themselves, even in formal parliaments where each representative speaks his "large golee" in defense of self-interest and at the expense of "commune profyt"; it is no wonder that Chaucer's parliament of birds continues to afford sympathetic amusement to the wise, and food for profitable meditation.

Index

Abraham, 80n
Absalom, 82n
Achitofel, 81, 82
Adam and Eve, 68, 114n, 123
adolescence, 13, 56, 69
Aeneas, 33, 47, 54
Aeneid, 46, 47
Africanus, 105-106, 108-111, 113, 144
ages of man, 13n
Alanus de Insulis, 5, 13-15, 20-21, 27, 36n, 42n, 43, 50n, 52n, 54n, 75n, 76n, 77n, 92n, 104n, 110n, 112, 115-116, 121n, 122, 124, 126, 141n, 145n
Albericus of London (Myth. Vat. III), 59n
Albertus Magnus, 125
Alcuin of York, 10
Alcyone, 35-41, 43-45, 47-48, 50, 52-53, 66-67, 69, 81, 90-91, 93, 95-96
alieniloquium, 17
Allegoriae in sacram scripturam, 27, 34n, 42n, 55n, 73n, 76n, 77n, 110n, 112n, 113n, 114n, 119n, 144n
allegory, 3-4, 6-8, 13, 15-17, 19, 22, 25-26, 30, 34n, 49, 53, 56, 66n, 94, 109, 116
Alexander, 80n
Altamura, A., 145n
alter ego, the poet's, 52-53, 57, 91
ambiguity, 95, 101
St. Ambrose, 45n
amicitia, 81n, 98, 102n. *See* love
Andreas Capellanus, 102, 120n
Angel, 123-124
Antenor, 81
Aray, 116-117
Aristotle, 17
Arnold, Matthew, 147
arrows of Cupid, 115-116, 145n
artifice vs. nature, 116-117
arts, 11, 12
Ascension, 91, 99

Athanasian Creed, 110n, 111, 113
aube, 40n
St. Augustine of Hippo, 5-10, 12, 17, 21-22, 29, 34n, 40n, 50n, 53n, 68n, 93-94, 112n
Augustinian, 13, 17, 19, 23, 29
authority, 132-133, 135
awakening, 38, 41, 44, 46, 55, 93, 97, 143-145

Bacchus and Ceres, 121
baptism, 112n
baptismal fonts, 50n
Bartholomeus Anglicanus, 8, 28
Bathsheba, 37
beard, 52
Beatrice, 70, 92-93, 95
beauty, 69, 79, 115; *of the flesh*, 70, 85, 91, 100, 118; *of the spirit*, 70-73, 75-76, 98, 99
bed, 42-43, 47-48, 108
Bede, 7, 10, 16-17, 29, 33, 34n, 42n, 49n, 73n, 76n
Beichner, P. E., 28, 84n
Bennett, J. A. W., 102n, 109n, 116n, 125n, 133n
bereavement, 37, 43, 46
Berchorius, Petrus (Pierre Bersuire), 8, 28, 40n, 50n, 52n, 118n, 119n, 135n, 138n
St. Bernard, 71, 136
Bestiary of Guillaume le Clerc, 49n
De bestiis et aliis rebus, 54, 77n
Bible (Douay Version), 6-8, 18, 21, 24-27, 29; *Gen. 1. 28*, 114n; *2 Kings 12. 22-23*, 37; *3 Kings 4. 23*, 49n; *Ps. 1*, 112, *6. 6*, 42n, *41. 1*, 49n, *44. 10*, 112n; *Eccles. 8. 1*, 76n, *9. 12*, 112n; *Wisd. 2. 1*, 75n, *7*, 145n, *7. 26*, 72, *8. 16*, 75n, *11. 13*, 75n; *Cant. 2. 12*, 136, *4. 12*, 110, 112, *4. 13-14*, 113, 114n, *4. 16*, 114n, *7. 4*, 76; *Matt. 3. 11*, 112n; *4. 10*, 112n, *10. 34*, 119n, *13. 13*, 77n, *20. 1-*

Index

16, 92n; *Mark 4. 21-22*, 71, *4.
38*, 42n; *Luke 7. 32*, 73n, *8. 16-
17*, 71; *John 1. 5*, 71, *11. 9*, 59n;
Acts 9. 33-34, 33n; *Rom. 13. 11-
13*, 40n; *1 Cor. 15. 34*, 40n; *2
Cor. 8. 21*, 71-72; *Eph. 5. 14*,
40n; *1 Thess. 5. 4-8*, 40n; *Apoc.
19. 17*, 123-124
birds, 43-45, 49, 56, 114, 123, 128,
140, 147
black (color), 42, 55, 99
Black Knight, 51-53, 55, 89, 91,
94, 97-100, 117
Black Prince, 42n
Blanche, Duchess of Lancaster,
34n, 35, 38, 45, 51-53, 72, 73n,
74, 77, 80, 83, 85, 88-89, 91-92,
94-100
bliss, 61, 63, 64, 103, 142. See joy
Boccaccio, 18-22, 24-25, 30, 90n,
116-117, 118n, 119, 121
Bode, G. H., 59n, 119n
body (flesh), 70-71, 73, 76, 83, 89
Boethius, 23, 29, 34n, 50, 53n, 60n,
62, 69, 103, 108n
St. Bonaventura, 73n, 93
book, 43, 102, 104. See story
Bradwardine, Thomas, 40n
brass and copper, 118
Bromyard, John, 24, 28, 123n
Bronson, B., 109n
Brown, Carleton, 102n
Bruno of Asti, 59n
Brusnelli, G., and G. Vandelli,
15n
Bury, Richard de, 145n
Buttimer, C. H., 11
Byheste and Art, 119, 120n

Cain, Generation of, 84
cave, 36, 40-41, 44, 46
cavea, 123n
"Cecile," 25
Celestial City, *see* New Jerusalem
"certain thing," 104-105
chamber, 42, 44, 47-48, 95
charity, 9, 12, 22, 55, 65, 69, 71-
76, 83, 98, 105, 112, 122, 126, 147
chastity, 76, 121

Chaucer, *Book of the Duchess*, 3,
24, 30, 32-100, 101, 105, 109,
117; *Parliament of Fowls*, 3,
24, 30, 55n, 84, 101-147; *House
of Fame*, 3; *Legend of Good
Women*, 3, 47n; *Troilus*, 117;
Wife of Bath's Tale, 134n; *Second Nun's Tale*, 25; *Canon's
Yeoman's Tale*, 119n; *Parson's
Tale*, 35, 39n, 65n, 68n, 117n,
118n, 121n
chess, 35, 60, 63
childishness (*pueritia*), 13, 14,
68n, 70, 88
chivalry, 35, 134
Christ, 17, 19, 45-46, 64, 70-71, 75,
88, 112n
Christine de Pisan, 47n
Church, 46, 48, 60-61, 70-71, 97,
110-112, 114, 118
Cicero, 39-41, 105, 111
circumstances, 65, 82, 83
Col, Pierre, 47n
comedy, 4, 11-12, 147
"common profit," 105-108, 122,
125-126, 132, 134, 138-139
company, 69, 77
confession, 54, 57, 65, 67-69, 81-
82, 98, 100
Confirmation, 56
confusion, 132, 134. *See* noise
conscience, 43, 71
consolation, 38, 40, 43, 45, 50-51,
54-55, 58, 88-89, 92, 94-95, 97
contemplation, 42-43, 48, 90, 93,
96-97, 105, 144
core and rind, *see* fruit and chaff
Council of Trent, 28
courtesy, 35, 57, 116-117
crown without jewels, 77
cuckoo, 132-133, 138-139, 142, 147
Cupid, 103, 115-117, 142, 145n,
146
cupidity, 9-10, 55, 69, 98
cure, 50, 54, 58, 63, 96-97, 111,
114, 143. *See* remedy
curtain, 119

150

Index

Cytherea, 109, 146

Dalilah, 64
Dame Pees, 119
dance, 72-73
dancing women, 118
Daniel, 19
Dante, 15-16, 22-24, 40, 47, 53n, 70, 88, 92-95, 106n, 109n, 111, 113, 116
darkness, 144
Daunger, 112, 126
David, 37-38
Davy, M. M., 73n
dawn, 43-46, 49, 92, 99
day, 43-44, 58, 59n, 92, 99, 108, 114; cloudless, 44, 47, 48
Day of Judgment, 49, 106
death, 32, 35, 37-38, 41, 52, 57-59, 62, 64, 77, 81, 83-85, 87-90, 94-95, 98, 106, 113-114, 129
debate, 133, 135
De Bruyne, E., 72n
Dedalus, 58
Deduit, 55n
Delyt, 55n, 117
description of the lady, 70-71, 73n, 74-75, 77, 79-80, 87, 96
despair, 34, 35n, 36, 55, 57-58, 61-62, 77, 80-81, 84, 86, 88-90, 100, 117. See tristitia
destiny, 80
dialectic, 11
dialogue, 52, 65
Diana, 121
Dido, 64
discipline, 69
Disdain, 112, 126
distinctiones, 27
doctrine, 6, 10, 12, 28-29, 43, 47, 102, 105
dog, 48, 54, 97
domus Naturae, 115-117, 122
Donatus, 17
Douglas, Gavin, 102n
dove, 42, 119
dream, 30, 36, 38, 40n, 42-45, 47-53, 89, 92-93, 96, 99, 109-110
dreamer (as character), 43, 45-51,

53-57, 61-63, 65-67, 74, 79, 81-82, 88-89, 91, 97-99, 105, 121-124, 136
Dream of Scipio, 4, 105, 110, 113
Druce, G. C., 49n
duck, 135n, 137-138
Duenna, the, 117
dulness (taedium), 75
Dunbar, 4

eagles, see formel, fowls of ravine, merlin, royal eagle, tercelet
Easter, 99
Echo, 64
Edward III, 35
"eight year sickness," 32-33, 34n, 35, 47, 49-50, 54, 95
elegy, 94
"embosed," 48-50
Envy, 74
error, 55, 68
Esther, 77, 80n
eternal bliss, 106, 107
etymology, 17, 25
eulogy, 35, 51, 53, 96
example, Blanche's, 70, 76-77, 79, 84, 88, 96, 98; priestly, 54, 87; Seys', 96; Socrates', 63
exemplum, 19, 30
excuse, 80-81
exegesis, Scriptural, 5, 7, 16, 23, 25, 27, 29-30
eyes, 73-75, 77
Ezekiel, 19

fable, 11, 13, 16, 18, 20
face, 75-77
faith, 73, 88, 137; Christian, 94, 97-98, 110, 146
faithful of the Church, 111, 114n
fall of man, 68, 114, 122-123, 126, 128
feudal investiture, 88
fiction, 5, 12, 15, 18-20
field of Scriptures, 104
figure, 5-8, 12-13, 18, 22, 25-27, 34, 60, 63, 73n
fires of desire, 120

151

Index

fish, 112, 114
flesh, *see* body
flowers, 55, 113, 114n
flowery path, 51, 54
Foliot, Gilbert, 110n
Foolhardiness, 118
formel eagle, 126-130, 134, 140-142
Fortune, 3, 8, 50, 53, 59-62, 63n, 64, 69-70, 73, 98, 127
Fourth Lateran Council, 29
fowls of ravine, 125, 136
Froissart, 32
fruit, 112
fruit and chaff (and related figures), 5-8, 10, 13, 15, 19, 21-23, 104n
frustration, Priapic, 120, 122, 127-129, 137, 144, 145n
Fulgentius, 8, 25
Furnivall, F. J., 118n

Ganelon, 81
garden, 47, 55, 64n, 113, 116; of Nature, 116-117, 122-123, 144, 146; of Paradise, 110, 113; of the Church, 111, 112n, 113, 122
garlands, 120, 129-130
Garnerius of St. Victor, 28, 54n
gates, 110-113
Gaylord, Alan, 134n
"gentilesse," 117, 134
Gerson, Jean, 47n
Gesta Romanorum, 49n
gift of Fortune, 40n, 50, 53, 60, 69, 103, 118, 127; of God, 127
Gilbert of Hoyland, 74n, 76n
gloss, 44, 46-47, 50
Glossa ordinaria, 33n, 64n, 76n, 84n
gluttony, 121
God of Love, 74, 101, 106-107, 113
gold, 42, 72-73
Goldschmidt, A., 123n
good works, 4, 35, 73, 88
goose, 132, 135-137, 139, 147
Gower, 65n
Grace, 53, 97, 140-141, 144
grain of faith, 104

grammar, 11
grass, 55
Green, R. H., 16n
green walls, 110, 118
St. Gregory the Great, 16n, 28-29, 45n, 49n, 56n, 73n, 106n, 112n
grief, 36-38, 41, 48, 50-52, 55-59, 62, 64-65, 67-68, 73, 76, 81-83, 86, 90-91
Grivot, D., and G. Zarnecki, 110n
guide, 77, 90, 127

Hades, 35
hair, golden, 72-73, 121
Halm, C., 16n, 17n
happiness, 81
harmony, 45-46, 56n, 84, 106, 114, 123-125, 128, 132, 143; of Nature, 126, 128, 143-144
Harrowing of Hell, 32n
Hart, T. R., 108n
hart, 48-50, 53-54, 57-58, 62, 91, 97
heart, 39, 49-50, 53, 57, 62, 66, 68, 70-71, 73-75, 78, 80, 83, 85-87, 96-97, 100, 108
Hell, 35n, 41, 44
Henry of Lancaster, 34n
herbs, 114
heresy, 82
Hilberg, I., 38n
hill of Nature, 124; of sand, 119
history, 11, 18
Hoccleve, 4
Hoeppfner, E., 69n
Holkot, Robert, 25, 40n
Holy Spirit, 21, 112
Homer, 18
Honorius of Autun, 92n, 112n, 114n
hope, 77, 92, 97-98
horn, 48, 50n, 97
horse, 49, 50n, 97
hortus conclusus, 110, 113. See garden
hound, 53-54
Hugh of St. Victor, 10-13, 15, 20-21, 28-29, 38n, 47, 103-104, 105n, 107, 108n

152

Index

humility, 78, 80, 132
humor, 3, 98, 102n, 146-147
hunt, 48-50, 53-54, 58, 62, 83, 89, 91-92, 97, 100
hunter, 48-49; *see* Octovyen
Huppé, B. F., 4n, 5n, 10n, 62n, 133n, 144n
husband, 37, 41, 48
husk and kernel, *see* fruit and chaff
hypocrisy, 71, 74, 117, 132, 138

Icelos, 40n
idleness, 35, 68-69, 84, 97
idol, 59, 130, 136
idolatry, 39, 47, 62, 64, 83, 129, 137-138, 141, 144
ignorance, 78
illumination, 93, 97
illusion, 41
imagination, 94-95, 103
immortality of the soul, 106
"increase and multiply," 114n, 122-123, 126-127, 135
innocence, 68-69, 72, 76, 78, 80
inspiration, 35, 53, 99
intellect, 5, 8, 61-62, 78, 88, 97, 105
intellectual exercise, 10, 14, 20, 21
interpretation, 6-7, 12, 22-26, 30, 43, 97
Isaiah, 19
Isidore of Seville, 7, 10, 17, 25, 34n, 115
Itinerarium mentis in Deum, 93

Jean de Meun, 22
jealousy, 128
Jelosye, the goddess, 120-122, 130
St. Jerome, 29, 38
Job, 80n
John of Gaunt, 51-53, 88n
St. John, 91
John the Scot, 10, 35
Joseph, 43, 97
joy, 74, 90, 92, 103
Juan Ruiz, 108n, 117, 120
Judith, 80n

Juno, 36, 39-42, 66
justice, 78

Keil, H., 17n
kernel and shell, *see* fruit and chaff
Kittredge, G. L., 57
knight, 14, 56
knowledge, 68
Koonce, B. G., 123n
Krautheimer, R., 50n

Lactantius, 77n
lady, 33, 56, 58, 61-62, 67, 69-70, 72-77, 79-89, 91-92, 94, 96, 98-100
lamb, 17, 23, 123
Lamech, 84
Lauds, 46, 92, 99
laughter, 71-73
Laura, 25, 92
law of Nature, 35, 115, 123; of God, 105, 123, 126
leaves, 112, 114
lechery, 116-118, 121
Lecoy, F., 108n
Lethean streams, 41
letter, 5-6, 10-13, 15, 23
light, 47-48, 59n, 70-71, 73, 92, 98, 113-114, 138, 144
"likerous folk," 112
Lindsay, W. M., 17n
lion, 17, 23
literary theory, 3-4, 6-7, 10, 18, 22
"long castle" (Lancaster), 91-92
look, 69-70, 74, 86
Loomis, R. S., 34n
lore and lust, 105
love, 8-10, 32, 67-68, 70, 73, 75, 79, 80-84, 86, 87-88, 93, 98; Ch. III, *passim*
lover, 32-33, 47, 68, 95, 108, 118, 138
Lubac, Henri de, 5, 13n
Lucrece, 80
lux divinae cognitionis, 44-45
Lydgate, 4, 121n

McCall, J. P., 123n

153

Index

McKisack, M., 125n
Machaut, 69n, 78n, 80n
Macrobius, 4, 43, 109-110, 146
magister, 133
Manfred of Sicily, 60-61
manor, 78
marriage, 88n, 127, 137, 143-144; as symbol, 124; to Christ, 123
Marrou, H. I., 5n, 6-7, 8n
St. Martin of Leon, 123n
"mased," 32, 35, 38, 50, 53-54
Massera, A. F., 25
mate, 126-128, 130, 142
mating, 137, 140, 142-143; of fowls, 123-124, 128
maturity, 13-14, 99
May, 43-46, 49, 112
meadow, 113
Medea, 64
medicines, 111
meditation, 104-105, 108-109
Meditationes, 107n
meed, 118
melody, 84; *see* harmony
memory, 45, 81, 88-92, 99, 108
mercy, 74, 78, 85
merlin, 139
message, 37-38, 40n, 41, 44, 50, 110-111
Messagerye, 118
messenger, 36, 40n, 41, 44, 50, 110-111
metals of Venus, 118. *See* brass and copper
mind, 40, 45, 71, 95, 97
miracle, 101
mirror, 78, 81
mistress, 32
moderation, 141
modesty, 118
moon and stars, 70
Morpheus, 36, 39-42, 44, 46, 48
Moses, 73n
music of the spheres, 114

narrative, 11
Nature, 5, 36, 56-57, 68, 85, 114, 122, 124-130, 133, 137, 139-143, 147

Nature's design, 125, 134, 137, 141
neck, 76
Neckam, Alexander, 25, 59n, 138n
New Jerusalem, 9, 46, 69n, 72, 91-92, 98
New Law, 8
night, 59n, 108, 144
Noah's Ark, 66n
Noema, 84
noise, 124-125, 131-132, 144
"north-north-west," 109

oak, 51, 55, 117
obscurity, 6, 12, 20
Octovyen, 48-49, 89, 91, 97, 98, 100
Oliver, 82
Olson, Paul A., 126n
Orpheus, 15, 58
Osgood, C. G., 19n, 22
Ovid, 8, 15, 25, 37n, 39, 40n, 58, 66n, 120
Ovide Moralisé, 25, 41n
owl, 138

Pantin, W. A., 40n, 65n
parable, 19, 30
Paradise, 54, 64n, 110-115, 143
Paré, G., 8n
park, 108-109
Parliament, 125-126, 134, 144
patience, 119
pearls, 14, 21-22
peace, 43, 46, 48, 81, 96, 120, 139
penance, 42n, 96
Penelope, 80
persona, 34n
Peter of Blois, 73n, 82n, 87n, 102n
Peter of Riga, 28
Peter Quivil, 117n
Peter the Lombard, 28, 42n, 49n, 50n, 64n
Petrarch, 16-18, 21, 23, 25, 53n, 59n, 90n, 92
Phantasos, 40n
phantasy, 32, 40
Phenix, 77

154

Index

philosophy, 4, 11-12, 14, 20, 23, 29-30, 36, 38, 50, 103-105, 145n
Phyllis, 64
physician, 32-35, 41, 43-45, 47, 50, 58-59, 61, 84, 88, 90-96, 98-99
Piers Plowman, 23-24, 115
pigs, 6, 14, 21
pilgrimage, 9, 47
pillars of jasper, 118
pillow, 42
Pitra, J. B., 28
Pleasaunce, 116-117
poet (as character), 34, 38-39, 42-45, 47-48, 50, 52, 54-55, 88, 91-93, 96-97, 99, 108-109, 113, 115-116
poem, 4-5, 7-8, 11-12, 16-21, 23-27, 29-31
positive law, 127-128
praise of God, 48, 73, 90, 97-99, 114, 143
prayer, 36, 42
preacher, 53
precept and counsel, 56, 69, 70
Priapus, 120-122, 129, 145n
priest, 54
principles of consent, 140
pride, 117
Providence, 65, 81
Prudentius, 22
psychology, 50
pun, 46, 49
punishment, 107, 111
Purgatory, 148

quadrivium, 8
queen, 122; in chess, 60-61, 63-65
Queen Philippa, 3
quies vitae, 34n

Rabanus Maurus, 8, 10, 25, 27-28, 42n, 49n, 70, 73n, 75n, 78n, 82n, 106n, 110n, 113n, 144n
radiance, 71, 76, 100
reading, 43, 96, 104-105, 145
reason, 60, 62, 63n, 69, 76, 108, 118, 140, 141
red and white, 75
Red Sea, 73n

remedy, 73, 112, 128
repentance, 64, 68, 81-82
répertoires exégetiques, 27
rest, 108
Resurrection, 45-46, 49, 50n, 77, 89-93, 97-98
reward of the just, 92, 99
revelation, 146
rhetoric, 7, 16, 19, 104
Richard II, 51
Richesse, 120
"rich hill" (Richmond), 91-92
Ridewall, John, 25
ring, 88
river, 113
Robert de Sorbon, 117n
Robert Mannyng, 118n
Robertson, D. W., 47n, 50n, 62n, 73n, 117n, 118n
Robinson, F., 23n
rocks, 40-41, 44
Roland, 82
Roman de la rose, 22, 25, 30, 44, 46-47, 55n, 60, 63, 74, 112, 117
romance, 35
Roncaglia, A., 118n
roof, 43
room, see chamber
Rossi, V., 17n
royal eagle, 126, 129-131, 134, 137, 141-142
Rudisill, G., 123n
Rupert of Deutz, 114n

saints, 70-71
Samson, 64
satire, 11
sceptre, 120
Scheler, A., 32n
Scipio, 105-106, 109-111, 113, 115, 145-146
seedfowl, 125, 132, 136, 142
sense, level of, 10-11, 13-15, 17, 23, 30, 43, 72, 143
sentence, 10-11, 23-25, 30, 38, 68, 93-94, 104-106, 108, 110-111, 132
servant of Venus, 130
Seys (Ceyx), 36-39, 40n, 41, 43-45, 47, 53, 63, 90, 93, 95-96

Index

shadows, 55
sighs, 120, 123, 130, 145
simile, 63
sin, 54, 64
singing, 43, 45, 72-73
Singleton, C. S., 16n, 24, 93
sinner, 38, 43
Sion, 91
Sisyphus, 59
Skeat, W. W., 81
Skogan, 4
sleep, 32, 34-35, 39-41, 43, 45, 93, 96-97, 105, 109
sloth, 36, 80
Socrates, 62
solas, 104
"solempne servise," 43-46
Solomon, 80n
Solomon's Temple, 42, 64n
song, 11, 56-57, 84, 114, 143-144
Song of Songs, 46
sparrowhawk, 136
speaker (as character), 5, 32-33, 34n, 35, 37-38, 41, 43, 52, 55, 58, 69, 90, 92-93, 95, 97
speech, 71, 72, 73, 76-77
Spenser, 22
"speres thryes thre," 84, 106
Spicq, C., 5, 27
spring, 45, 144
Spurgeon, C. F., 4n
squirrel, 25
Stahl, W. H., 4n
stars, 122
Stearns, M. W., 34n
Stillwell, G., 109n
story, 4, 36-37, 39, 43-47, 90, 93, 95-96
summer, 144, 147
sun, 44, 46-48, 70, 122
symbol, 6-8, 22-24, 26-30, 33, 42-46, 49, 53-57, 68, 73, 76-78, 91-92, 95-97, 99, 107, 110, 113, 115, 118, 145

Tantalus, 62
tapestry, 42
temperance, 74-75, 78
temperate day, 44, 47-48, 114

temple, 78; door of, 119; of God, 119; of Venus, 116-119, 122, 126, 137, 139, 145n
tercel, the second, 130; the third, 131
tercelet of the falcon, 133-134, 138, 140
Terence, 121
theme, 75, 95-96, 101, 108, 126
theology, 16-18, 28-30
Theseus, 121
thought, 68, 70
torch, 77, 109
torpor, 119
tower of ivory, 76
"town of Tewnes," 44, 46, 56
tragedy, 11
Toynbee, P. J., 15n
treasure, 73
tree, 18, 51, 53, 55, 97, 112-113, 124
Tree of Charity, 115; of Life, 115
tribulation, 76
tristitia, 35, 55, 59
Trivet, Nicholas, 29, 50, 62
trivium, 8
Troilus, 41
Trota Conventos, 117
Troy, 44, 81
truthfulness, 78
Tubal, 84
Tubalcain, 84
turtle dove, 132-133, 136-137, 139
tyrannical rule of love, 102
tyrant, 78

understanding, 105
use, abuse, and enjoyment, 9, 82n
Usk, 4

St. Valentine, 123, 128, 144, 147; day, 123-124; poem, 109, 143, 146-147
Venus, 84, 121-122, 126, 127, 128-130, 142-144, 147
De vera et falsa poenitentia, 68n
Vergil, 8, 18, 113, 146
Virgin Mary, 78
virtue, 70-71, 73, 76-77, 79-83,

Index

86-90, 93-94, 97-98, 111, 113, 129, 137
virtues and vices, 126-127
vision, 19, 30, 37, 40-41, 92-93, 97-99, 105, 109, 115, 143
voice of the turtle, 136
vow, 42, 66-67, 96

Walsingham, Thomas, 25
wall, 121; of faith, 118
waterfowl, 125, 132, 135-136, 141-142
waters of grace, 114
Well of Cupid, 115; of Grace, 111, 113, 115
whelp, 51, 53-55
white (color), 42, 72, 76, 99; table, 68, 69n; walls, 91
widows, 36
wife, 36, 41, 127, 129; of Bath, 132
Wilkins, David, 117n
will, 39, 61-62, 66-67, 69-70, 78,

81, 83, 97-98, 115, 116, 118, 122, 129
Wille, Cupid's daughter, 115
Wilmart, A., 27
wind, 114
windows, 44, 46, 48, 99
wisdom, 41, 50, 71, 75-76, 79, 86, 103-105, 108, 113, 145
wit, 66-68, 70, 80, 85-86
woods, 51, 54
words and things, 6-7, 27
world, 75
worm, 17, 23
wormfowl, 125, 132, 138, 142
wounds of sin, 111

year, 86, 99
youth, 13-14, 68-70, 79-80, 88, 97-99
Youthe, 118

Zorzi, D., 30n